Business Guides on the Go

"Business Guides on the Go" presents cutting-edge insights from practice on particular topics within the fields of business, management, and finance. Written by practitioners and experts in a concise and accessible form the series provides professionals with a general understanding and a first practical approach to latest developments in business strategy, leadership, operations, HR management, innovation and technology management, marketing or digitalization. Students of business administration or management will also benefit from these practical guides for their future occupation/careers.

These Guides suit the needs of today's fast reader.

Jan Y. Yang • Yunyi Gu • Zi Ling Tan

Chinese Electric Vehicle Trailblazers

Navigating the Future of Car Manufacturing

Jan Y. Yang
Simon-Kucher & Partners
Frankfurt am Main, Germany

Zi Ling Tan
Simon-Kucher & Partners
Berlin, Germany

Yunyi Gu
Simon-Kucher & Partners
Frankfurt am Main, Germany

ISSN 2731-4758 ISSN 2731-4766 (electronic)
Business Guides on the Go
ISBN 978-3-031-25144-3 ISBN 978-3-031-25145-0 (eBook)
https://doi.org/10.1007/978-3-031-25145-0

This Springer imprint is published by the registered company Springer Nature Switzerland AG
The registered company address is: Gewerbestrasse 11, 6330 Cham, Switzerland

Acknowledgement

The writing of this book would not have been possible without the blessing of our company Simon-Kucher & Partners Strategy & Marketing Consultants. We are lucky to build upon the rich body of knowledge in the relevant domains that has accrued at Simon-Kucher over years.

Special thanks go to Dr. Martin Gehring, Head of Global Automotive Practice at Simon-Kucher, who has encouraged us and trusted us with the opportunity to create this book.

We are obliged to our dear colleagues Brie Casazza and Lewis Hawes, who have worked tirelessly to polish our writing and elevate the quality of our book.

Last but not least, our gratitude goes to our editors Dr. Prashanth Mahagaonkar and Jialin Yan at Springer, who have supported us throughout the journey with their feedback and genuine interest.

Contents

List of Figures

List of Tables

1

Chinese EV Players: From Followers to Trailblazers

Keywords Electrification • Chinese electric vehicle Industry • Electric vehicle innovations • Powertrain shift • Future of mobility

Made in China, no wonder.

I still remember laughing with my friends over the pair of Bluetooth earphones I'd bought on AliExpress for 20 euros, which had inexplicably ceased to function in just 2 weeks. It was not too long ago when the label "Made in China" was synonymous with low quality and fake products. Electronics, textiles, plastics—you name it. It is not too surprising, especially when you consider how rapidly the Chinese manufacturing industry has grown. China accounted for 28.7% of global manufacturing output in 2019 (Richter 2022) and 30.0% in 2021 (Xinhua 2022).

This perception prevailed in the automotive industry, where most attempts by Chinese automakers to expand globally were met with resounding failure. However, times have changed, and apprehension toward Chinese products and vehicles has eroded. China's rise as an economic superpower and its steely determination related to electrification has propelled it to the forefront of the automotive industry, where it is

© The Author(s), under exclusive license to Springer Nature Switzerland AG 2023
J. Y. Yang et al., *Chinese Electric Vehicle Trailblazers*, Business Guides on the Go,
https://doi.org/10.1007/978-3-031-25145-0_1

now ready to challenge the existing leaders. This is the story of Chinese electric vehicle (EV) trailblazers and how they will shape the future of mobility.

In May 2021, William Li, CEO of one of China's growing electric EV start-ups, NIO, announced the company's first venture in entering international markets. Setting up shop in Norway, NIO aims to enter the wider European market from 2022 (Mihalascu 2021). Li is not alone. NIO is one of many Chinese EV start-ups that have found immense success at home and are now setting their sights abroad: first stop—Europe.

As more and more EV start-ups start looking overseas for opportunities, especially within the European market, it is time for established manufacturers to gain a better understanding of who they are dealing with and start contemplating their own moves to stave off their competitors from the Far East.

> "The next Golf must not be a Tesla!
> The next Golf must not come from China!
> The next icon must again be a Wolfsburger! Trinity!"
>
> *- Former Volkswagen Chairman Herbert Diess*

These were the fighting words of former Volkswagen chairman Herbert Diess when speaking to disgruntled workers after facing a vote of no-confidence back in November 2021 (Wittich 2021). A long-time admirer of Tesla, Diess found himself in trouble with the works council when he suggested that Volkswagen was at risk of losing 30,000 jobs if it did not step up production. It is not the prettiest reality for traditional automakers to face, but Diess has acknowledged that Volkswagen has fallen behind their competitors when it comes to the race for electrification.

He recognizes that this new era in the automotive industry revolves around technology and software and requires a different set of competencies that Volkswagen just does not have right now. Their productivity lags behind the likes of Tesla—Volkswagen needs more than 30 h to produce a car at its main plant, while Tesla only needs 10 h. Diess sees Tesla as the benchmark for the future that is here to stay, but also admitted that Chinese EVs were "really good" (Lambert 2021).

This book informs readers about the latest technological developments and advancements that have taken place in China and offers ideas as to what Chinese newcomers will bring with them when they arrive on the scene.

1.1 Electrification Across the World

Electrification seems to be the new trend of the present day. While the adoption of EVs is speeding up worldwide, the Chinese market has exhibited the most growth. For the first time in history, Chinese automakers are presenting a serious challenge to traditional Western brands. Global EV sales reached 6.75 million units in 2021, a 108% increase from the previous year. Even if the numbers are inflated because of the pandemic causing a low baseline for sales in 2020, it represents a return to the positive trend EVs had previously enjoyed. Total light vehicle sales only recovered by 4.6% in 2021, meaning the global market share of EVs almost doubled from 4.2% to 8.3%. China exhibited the most growth, as EV sales increased by 155% from the previous year, and the market share increased from 5.5% to 13.3%. Meanwhile in Europe, EV sales increased by 66% from the previous year, with the market share increasing from 10% to 17% (Irle 2022).

Unless stated otherwise, "EV" is always used to refer to both battery electric vehicles (BEVs) and plug-in hybrid electric vehicles (PHEVs) throughout this book. BEVs operate entirely on electric motors. PHEVs have both an electric motor and an internal combustion engine (ICE), and the battery can be charged via an external plug. EVs do not include hybrid electric vehicles (HEVs). HEVs also have both an electric motor and an ICE, but the battery cannot be charged via an external plug. As a result, they have shorter ranges on electric power and rely more heavily on the ICE.

China leads the way in the adoption of EVs, with more than half of all EV sales being made in China, as seen in Fig. 1.1 (Irle 2022). This number looks set to grow, as investments in infrastructure, performance, and subsidies incentivize the Chinese population to go electric. The rapid

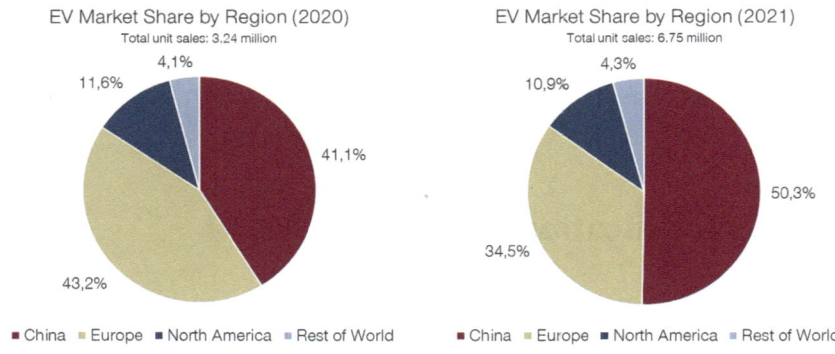

Fig. 1.1   Market share for EVs by region in 2020 and 2021 (Irle 2022)

growth and development of EV producers within China will only push this number higher. The Chinese government has announced that EVs should make up 40% of new vehicles sold by 2030, and the government continues to take steps toward this goal.

1.2   Driving Forces and Recent Developments

There are several driving forces behind the rise of the EV industry. This revolution has been brought about as the world looks for ways to limit the effects of climate change in line with the 2015 Paris Agreement. At the talks in Paris, traditional ICE vehicles were seen as a large contributor to carbon emissions, and as such, governments started looking for more sustainable alternatives such as EVs.

One particular obstacle to the widespread adoption of EVs in the past was their poor range, coupled with the lack of charging infrastructure. However, as technology continues to improve and both the private sector and governments invest more in the industry, these fears are being alleviated. From a consumer perspective, the ever-improving performance of EVs has made them comparable to or even better than ICE vehicles in certain respects.

Chinese automakers have taken the limitations of the EV, such as poor range and long charging times, and circumvented them successfully

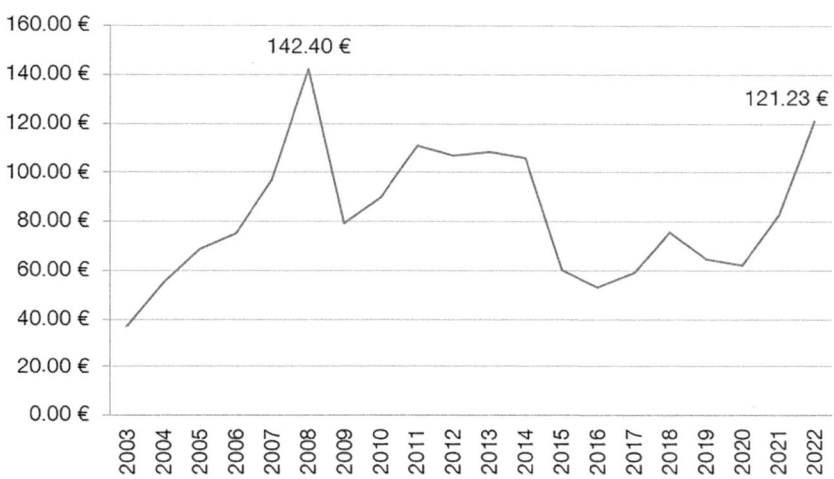

Fig. 1.2 Daily price per barrel of crude oil (EUR) (Armstrong 2022)

within the domestic market. For example, Chinese automaker NIO offers batteries as a service (BaaS), with hundreds of battery-swapping stations across China that allow consumers to switch to a fresh battery in a matter of minutes.

A more recent event fueling the adoption of EVs is the rise in fuel costs. As seen in Fig. 1.2 (Armstrong 2022), oil prices skyrocketed to a peak of approximately 142 euros (EUR) in 2008, as demand surged while production stagnated. This was one of the factors that helped accelerate the development of EVs. Following the COVID-19 pandemic, demand for fuel has soared once again, as manufacturing and international travel have started back up again. The already rising prices have been compounded by war between Ukraine and Russia, the latter of which is a major oil supplier, especially to the European Union. Between June 2021 and June 2022, the price of gas has risen by 48.7% in the USA, while the price of electricity has risen by 12% (Martin 2022). This trend has been mirrored across the world. As EVs continue to become more efficient, consumers may find them more economically viable; especially considering the variety of available governmental subsidies.

1.3   Competitive Landscape

While Western automakers have always been the biggest players when it comes to vehicles with combustion engines thanks to their strong legacy and deep expertise, the trend toward electrification in recent years has ushered Chinese automakers onto center stage in the automobile industry. The electrification of vehicles provided the automakers, big and small alike, with the opportunity to start on new ground and make a name for themselves. Even though Western companies have built up their reputation over decades selling traditional ICE vehicles, when it comes to the race for electrification, every brand, no matter its history, begins at the same starting line.

Chinese automakers have gained massive success on their home turf, outflanking established players. Domestically, Chinese automakers dominate the market—in 2021, only Tesla made it into the top 10 EV models in China by sales volume (Muyu 2022)—while globally, eight out of the 25 biggest automakers by market cap are Chinese (Yahoo Finance 2022).

The total market share of major Chinese automakers worldwide increased from 19% in 2020 to 24.3% in 2021 as seen in Table 1.1 (Pontes 2022), with automotive giant BYD leading the charge. They have gained ground against long-time market leader Tesla, whose market share has dropped in recent years, as it faces stiffer competition. As more and more automakers set their sights abroad, it is high time for established manufacturers to get a better understanding of who they are dealing with.

Building on a strong foundation rooted in China's booming EV market and enabled by governmental investment and support, Chinese EV players are increasing their efforts to penetrate international markets—and Europe is often their primary target. The timing could not be better for ambitious upstarts to initiate their growth ambitions.

Traditionally, the European market has been difficult for international automakers to penetrate, and while this may still hold true, the horizon looks a bit different now, and Chinese automakers see an opportunity to replicate their domestic success. Chinese EVs are already infiltrating the European market. The first Chinese start-up to go on sale in Europe was Aiways, which launched its fully electric U5 SUV in August 2020. They

Table 1.1 Top 25 automakers by market cap (truncated) (Pontes 2022)

1	Tesla	🇺🇸
2	Toyota	🇯🇵
3	BYD	🇨🇳
11	Great Wall Motors	🇨🇳
12	NIO	🇨🇳
13	Li Auto	🇨🇳
15	SAIC	🇨🇳
18	Xpeng	🇨🇳
21	Geely	🇨🇳
23	Changan	🇨🇳

Pure EV players

were closely followed by XPeng, which delivered its G3 smart electric SUV model to Norway in December 2021. MG, a subsidiary of China's SAIC Motor, is already selling its cars in 14 European countries. Europe is a promising landscape for newcomers and future contenders—such as BYD and Geely—to achieve fast market growth.

1.4 Outlook

A report by Research and Markets in 2021 projected that the automotive industry would grow at a compound annual growth rate[1] (CAGR) of 3.71% from 2020 to 2030 (Research and Markets 2021a, b). Within a similar period, the EV industry is forecasted to grow at a CAGR of 26.8% (Research and Markets 2021a, b). It is obvious that electrification will have a predominant role to play in the future of mobility.

As automakers enter the EV market, to differentiate themselves from their competitors, they need to look beyond just performance and carbon emissions. There is still room to create value within this market, and Chinese automakers are leading in this effort.

This book will explore how Chinese automakers are turning the humble car into a smart, multifunctional terminal, how advanced driver assistance systems (ADAS) could be the way forward, and how producers can deal with a major consumer concern—range anxiety. By exploring the possibilities that software and hardware offer, companies can develop an attractive value proposition for their customers.

This book will also dive into marketing, sales, and pricing strategies employed by Chinese automakers and provide a current overview as well as an outlook into the future of the EV industry.

References

Armstrong M (2022) Infographic: oil price surges to highest since 2008. Statista Infographics. https://www.statista.com/chart/27000/brent-crude-barrel-price-timeline/. Accessed 23 Aug 2022

Irle R (2022) EV-volumes—the electric vehicle world sales database. Ev-volumes.com https://www.ev-volumes.com/country/total-world-plug-in-vehicle-volumes/. Accessed 23 Aug 2022

---

[1] Compound annual growth rate is the mean annual growth rate over a specified period.

Lambert F (2021) VW CEO explains why it needs to be more like tesla: giga Berlin will produce 90 cars/hour on 1 line. Electrek https://electrek.co/2021/11/05/vw-ceo-explains-why-be-more-like-tesla-giga-berlin-manufacturing/. Accessed 23 Aug 2022

Martin E (2022) Inflation continues to rise—and gas prices are up nearly 50% since last year. cnbc.com. https://www.cnbc.com/2022/06/10/inflation-continues-to-rise-gas-prices-up-nearly-50percent-since-last-year.html#:~:text=Gas%20prices%20in%20particular%20are,U.S.%20overall%2C%20according%20to%20AAA. Accessed 23 Aug 2022

Mihalascu D (2021) NIO rumored to enter the United States market in 2025. InsideEVs. https://insideevs.com/news/604685/nio-rumored-enter-united-states-market-2025/. Accessed 23 Aug 2022

Muyu X (2022) 「数据报告」2021年新能源乘用车企业/车型销量一览 | 电车汇 ("Data Report" 2021 new energy passenger car companies/models sales list). Evhui.com. https://evhui.com/124957.html. Accessed 23 Aug 2022

Pontes J (2022) Electric car sales: global top 20—as of May 2022. CleanTechnica. https://cleantechnica.com/2022/06/29/electric-car-sales-global-top-20/. Accessed 23 Aug 2022

Research and Markets (2021a) Global automotive market, growth & forecast, impact of coronavirus, industry trends, by region, opportunity company analysis. researchandmarkets.com https://www.researchandmarkets.com/reports/5447681/global-automotive-market-growth-and-forecast. Accessed 23 Aug 2022

Research and Markets (2021b) Global electric vehicle market by component, vehicle (passenger cars, CV), propulsion (BEV, PHEV, FCEV), vehicle drive type (FWD, RWD, AWD), vehicle top speed (125 mph), charging point, vehicle class, V2G, and region—forecast 2030. researchandmarkets.com. https://www.researchandmarkets.com/reports/5337979/global-electric-vehicle-market-by-component. Accessed 23 Aug 2022

Richter F (2022) Infographic: China is the World's manufacturing superpower. Statista Infographics. https://www.statista.com/chart/20858/top-10-countries-by-share-of-global-manufacturing-output/. Accessed 23 Aug 2022

Wittich H (2021) VW-Boss Diess auf der Mitarbeiter-Versammlung: "Der nächste Golf darf kein Tesla sein!". auto motor und sport. https://www.auto-motor-und-sport.de/verkehr/vw-boss-diess-naechste-golf-darf-kein-tesla-sein/. Accessed 23 Aug 2022

Xinhua (2022) China accounts for 30% of global manufacturing output: Official. The State Council Information Office. http://english.scio.gov.cn/pressroom/2022-06/14/content_78269516.htm#:~:text=China%20accounted%20for%2030%20percent,the%20industry%20regulator%20showed%20Tuesday. Accessed 23 Aug 2022

Yahoo Finance (2022). Finance.yahoo.com. https://finance.yahoo.com/. Accessed 23 Aug 2022

2

The History of the Chinese EV Industry

Keywords Government subsidies • Five-year plan • Electric vehicle policies • Government incentives • Electric vehicle credits • Foreign entry barriers

As briefly touched on in Chap. 1, the EV industry in China is booming. In 2021, China overtook Europe as the world's leader in EV sales, and it shows no signs of slowing down. As of June 2022, approximately 26% of vehicles sold in China are BEVs and PHEVs (Kane 2022). For comparison, this number was 21% in Europe and 16% worldwide, showing how widespread the adoption of EVs has been in China. Chinese automakers have also gained ground in the rest of the world, with BYD currently leading the EV industry in sales (BEVs and PHEVs combined).

Numerous factors have contributed to China's rise in the EV industry, as seen in Fig. 2.1 (He and Jin 2021a, b). The Chinese government is one such factor, as it was the first in the world to recognize the potential of EVs and outline several policies that would encourage adoption and expedite the growth of domestic players. To this day, the national

J. Y. Yang et al., *Chinese Electric Vehicle Trailblazers*, Business Guides on the Go, https://doi.org/10.1007/978-3-031-25145-0_2

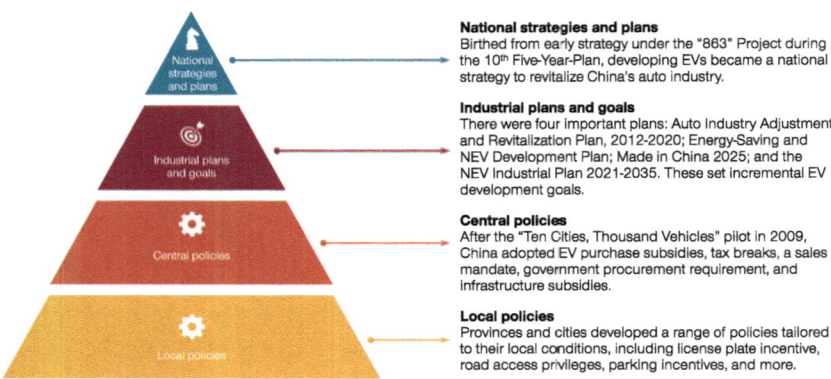

National strategies and plans
Birthed from early strategy under the "863" Project during the 10th Five-Year-Plan, developing EVs became a national strategy to revitalize China's auto industry.

Industrial plans and goals
There were four important plans: Auto Industry Adjustment and Revitalization Plan, 2012-2020; Energy-Saving and NEV Development Plan; Made in China 2025; and the NEV Industrial Plan 2021-2035. These set incremental EV development goals.

Central policies
After the "Ten Cities, Thousand Vehicles" pilot in 2009, China adopted EV purchase subsidies, tax breaks, a sales mandate, government procurement requirement, and infrastructure subsidies.

Local policies
Provinces and cities developed a range of policies tailored to their local conditions, including license plate incentive, road access privileges, parking incentives, and more.

Fig. 2.1 The policy architecture that supported the growth of the EV industry in China (He and Jin 2021b)

government continues to support the EV industry by laying out blueprints and policies that aim to boost the growth of the EV industry until it is no longer reliant on subsidies.

2.1   How the Chinese Government Fostered the EV Industry

The year 2009 marked an important milestone in the development of EVs in China, as the government recognized this technology's potential to increase economic growth and open the door for Chinese automakers to become global leaders. The Chinese government has formally established a national strategy for the development of new energy vehicles (NEVs). Since the 1990s, it has worked to put the country on a fast track to becoming a true global automotive powerhouse. But, as mentioned at the beginning of this book, the cars made in China were perceived as uncompetitive and of low quality. Almost all the best-selling mass-market cars in China were designed by Western companies and produced by joint ventures. The higher-end market was dominated by imported brands. The Chinese even coined the term ABB to refer to the German trio of Audi, Mercedes-Benz, and BMW, companies which are symbolic of premium cars.

However, Chinese automakers have made the most of this opportunity and benefited from the Chinese government's calculated and extensive support. From providing monetary incentives to creating the necessary infrastructure, the government has strategically equipped Chinese automakers with a unique vitality and business model that will allow them to triumph both domestically and abroad.

In the race toward electrification, the Chinese government invested nearly 880 million yuan renminbi (CNY) (about EUR 127 million) during the 10th 5-year plan to support a group of technologically capable automobile manufacturers and universities in forming partnerships, which has bred a unique Chinese mechanism of cooperation among government, industry, and academia, combining resources from all sectors of society (He and Jin 2021a, b). In 2008, the global financial crisis erupted. Oil prices soared, affecting the energy security of many economies, including that of China. The global crisis underlined the importance of energy security, which led to a strong desire to develop NEVs.

Before long, the Chinese government launched a large-scale pilot of NEVs, putting approximately 1000 NEVs on the roads in 10 cities, starting with fleets of city buses, sanitation and postal vehicles, and cabs, and gradually expanding to commercial and private vehicles. Monetary incentives followed, fueling the country's EV uptake and motivating automakers to join the race toward electrification long before their western competitors. Since the subsidies began in 2009 through to the end of 2021, CNY 100 billion (about EUR 14.5 billion) has been handed out to buyers including commercial fleet operators.

In the winter of 2013, the "great haze," a period in which smog enveloped much of the country, drew the attention of policymakers, especially in local government, to NEVs. Beijing initially launched a passenger car quota in 2011 as a control measure to address the city's traffic congestion problem, requiring users of new cars to obtain new car licenses through a lottery system, while EV drivers were exempted from the hassle. Other big cities followed suit soon after with similar measures to limit registrations of new cars with internal combustion engines. This measure to control the total number of passenger cars has produced a major incentive for consumers in big cities to purchase EVs. More importantly, while the total number of new license plates remained unchanged, the quota for NEV license plates was gradually increased to 60,000 over the following 3 years.

Local governments' policy innovations did not stop there: since 2013, the country has established an early warning system for heavy air pollution, and in 2015, Beijing issued its first red warning for heavy pollution (the highest level of the warning system) and began imposing restrictions on traditional fuel vehicles, allowing only vehicles with even or odd license plate numbers to operate in the city on alternating days, but exempting zero-emissions electric vehicles (ZEVs). These two local innovations (preferential licensing quotas for NEVs and traffic control exemptions) greatly stimulated consumer interest in EVs and quickly made Beijing one of the largest local markets for EVs in China. At the end of 2013, the number of NEVs in Beijing was only a few thousand, most of which were municipal buses deployed for the 2008 Summer Olympics. By 2017, that number had soared to 60,000 vehicles, two-thirds of which were private vehicles. From this period onward, EVs have taken on a third important mission in addition to revitalizing the national auto industry and improving national energy security: reducing air pollution.

Following Beijing, many Chinese municipalities increased investment in infrastructure, especially in public charging facilities to make travel using NEVs more convenient. Some cities have reduced costs for EV owners by waiving annual inspection fees and parking fees. Other cities have focused on promoting EV sharing, leasing, and other fleet solutions. In just 2 years from 2013 to 2015, China's annual sales of NEVs exploded from 18,000 to 330,000.

Leading the Way on Charging Infrastructure

The Chinese government has paved the way for future development growth by investing millions in charging infrastructure. The country is building ahead of demand, strategically installing public charging stations to meet future needs, in line with EV trends. In 2016, China surpassed Europe as the market with the most extensive public charging network worldwide and has continued to expand it at an impressive rate—installing as many as 112,000 public charging stations in December 2020 alone, more than the entire current U.S. network. In 2021, there were almost 1.2 million charging points, while the country in second place had less than 200,000, as seen in Fig. 2.2 (IEA 2022).

The Chinese government has no plans to stop there. By 2025, the aim is to ensure that at least 60% of expressway service stations in the country have rapid charging stations, rising to at least 80% in national ecological civilization pilot zones and key areas for air pollution prevention and control. The government will also strengthen maintenance and Internet services for charging facilities, ensure solid work in grid construction and energy supply, boost quality and safety supervision, and increase fiscal and financial support (NDRC 2022).

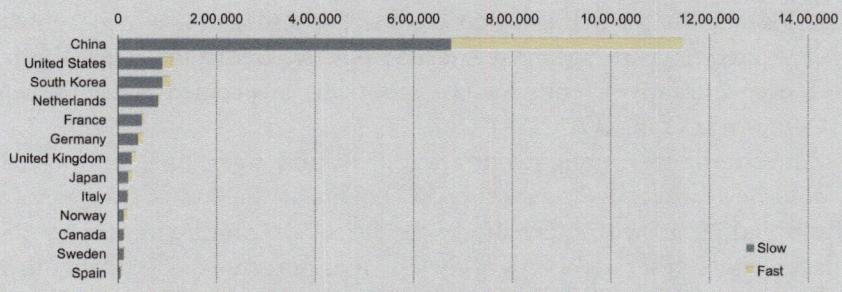

Fig. 2.2 Number of publicly available EV chargers (EVSE) in 2021, by major country and type (IEA 2022)

2.2   Moving Away from Subsidies Toward Self-Reliance

As EV sales boomed, EV subsidies started becoming costlier for the Chinese government. The technical requirements to qualify for the subsidies were too easy to meet, and fraud was rampant, as Chinese automakers were illegally registering vehicles to boost their sales numbers. The flaws in the policy design and implementation finally led to the Chinese government implementing a new plan in 2017. The subsidies were gradually phased out, with per-vehicle subsidies decreasing by 20% every year. Furthermore, the technical requirements were raised, and stronger anti-fraud and enforcement mechanisms were put in place. However, reports in 2022 indicate that the Chinese government is in talks with automakers to extend the subsidies to 2023 to keep the market growing, as the general economy has slowed down in large part due to the COVID-19 pandemic (Interesse 2022).

In place of the EV subsidies, the government implemented a credit system in 2017, which has further ensured the domestic EV market's continued growth. Partially modeled on California's pioneering Zero-Emission Vehicle (ZEV) program, the "dual-credit" policy is somewhat complicated (Chen and He 2022). Automakers gain credits for reducing the corporate average fuel consumption (CAFC) to below a certain level and lose credits for failing to do so. There is also a new energy vehicle (NEV) credit, where automakers receive positive credits for each EV produced and negative credits for not producing a specified percentage of EVs in a year (Yang 2021).

The criteria were designed in a way that most traditional automakers would have a negative total of CAFC credits at the end of the year. To avoid ending up with a penalty in the form of a production cap, automakers must either make EVs of their own or purchase credits from other companies. Automakers receive credits for each NEV produced. Regulators base credit targets for each automaker on its total production of passenger cars. The credits take various factors into consideration, such as the type of vehicle and its maximum speed, energy consumption, weight, and range. If an automaker does not reach the target, they must purchase credits from competitors to reach a surplus or face financial penalties.

This adjustment of national policies alludes to an important message: China's EV industry is slowly maturing. Now, the government is determined to move away from its initial strategic approach, which relied excessively on subsidies, government procurement, and entry barriers on products from international markets. Instead, the Chinese government is liberalizing its market and allowing for more market competition.

2.3   New Players in the Domestic Market

In their efforts to liberalize the market, the Chinese government announced that it would gradually remove foreign shareholding restrictions in the automotive industry beginning in mid-2018. Foreign companies producing EVs could now manufacture vehicles in China without having to form a joint venture with a Chinese company. The foreign equity ratio restriction (which requires foreign automakers to establish joint ventures with Chinese companies to invest in China, to hold no more than 50% of the shares in a venture, and to establish no more than two joint ventures in China for the same type of vehicle) has been in place since 1994 and has historically served to protect local Chinese automakers. The removal of this restriction demonstrated the Chinese government's confidence in the technological capabilities of local companies and unleashed the potential for more investment from international markets.

Prior to 2018, the share of purely foreign brands in China's NEV market was only about 5% (Wharton 2019). Just 1 month after the new regulations were implemented, Tesla announced the construction of a factory in Shanghai. The development of China's EV industry, the growing market size, and the increasingly liberal policy environment have convinced traditional automotive giants from around the world to cooperate with Chinese automakers in the NEV sector. BMW and Great Wall Motor joined forces to produce Mini-branded EVs in China. Toyota has also taken the opportunity presented by the development of EVs and the transformation of the mobility industry to establish partnerships with BYD and CATL, and the trend for global automotive companies to increase investment in China has clearly unfolded.

In addition to global players entering the local EV game, the Chinese EV industry has also witnessed the emergence and flourishing of domestic Chinese EV start-ups, which have demonstrated unprecedented innovation. The year 2018 saw a major milestone in the history of the Chinese EV industry when NIO became the first Chinese EV manufacturer to list on the New York Stock Exchange. Private sector brands such as BYD, NIO, and XPeng are increasingly gaining attention from the global automotive industry and represent the new powerhouse of Chinese auto manufacturing. Today, these companies are becoming some of the most successful fundraisers on global stock markets and are often seen as competitors to Tesla. This level of competitiveness has never been witnessed in China's traditional automotive industry. Having won the heart of the early adopters, the EV start-ups are now looking to scale up for the mass market and take on the established competitors.

2.4   Chinese EV Development in a Nutshell

Figure 2.3 He and Jin (2021a, b) illustrate the thrilling development of the Chinese EV industry with the strategies and specific policies of different periods (He and Jin 2021a, b). Clearly, Chinese automakers have made the most of the external factors put in place by the Chinese government long before any other country has done the same. These include monetary incentives, the credit system, and major investment in charging infrastructure. These factors have given Chinese automakers a leg up over their Western counterparts, as the rest of the world is only now moving toward this new norm. In the future, governmental support will decrease as the Chinese government looks to take a market-driven approach, but observers should not be surprised if the government steps in again should EV adoption start trending downward.

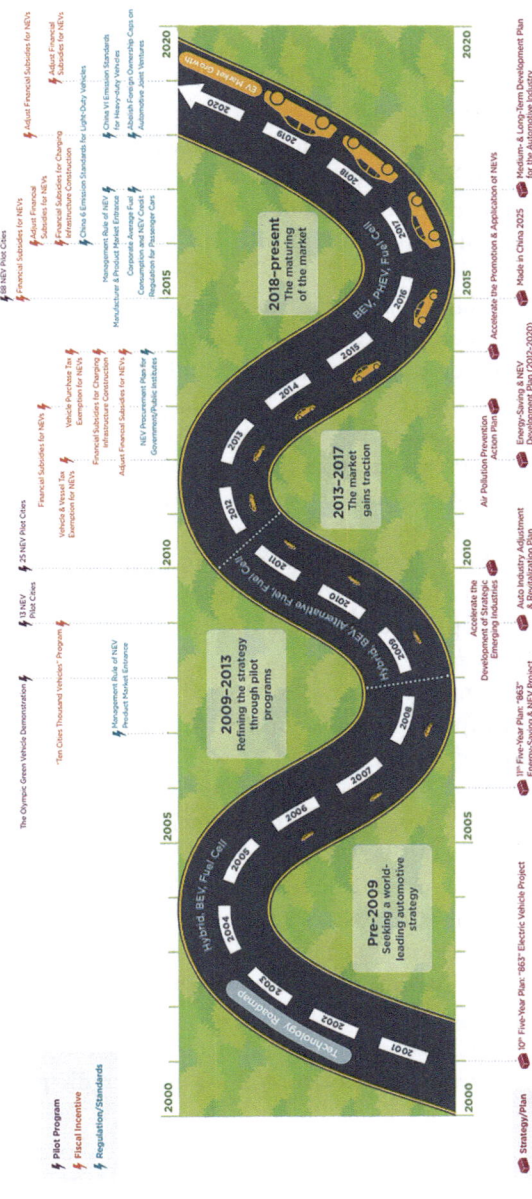

Fig. 2.3 Historical review of Chinese EV development (He and Jin 2021a)

References

Chen Z, He H (2022) How will the dual-credit policy help China boost new energy vehicle growth?. International Council on Clean Transportation. https://theicct.org/china-dual-credit-policy-feb22/. Accessed 23 Aug 2022

He H, Jin L (2021a) Driving a green future: a retrospective review of China's electric vehicle development and outlook for the future. Theicct.org. https://theicct.org/sites/default/files/publications/China-green-future-ev-jan2021.pdf

He H, Jin L (2021b) How China put nearly 5 million new energy vehicles on the road in one decade. International Council on Clean Transportation. https://theicct.org/how-china-put-nearly-5-million-new-energy-vehicles-on-the-road-in-one-decade/. Accessed 23 Aug 2022

IEA (2022) Publicly available EVSE chargers worldwide: country & type | Statista. Statista. https://www.statista.com/statistics/571564/publicly-available-electric-vehicle-chargers-by-country-type/. Accessed 23 Aug 2022

Interesse G (2022) China considers extending its EV subsidies to 2023. China Briefing News. https://www.china-briefing.com/news/china-considers-extending-its-ev-subsidies-to-2023/#:~:text=Moreover%2C%20Beijing%20revealed%20a%20plan,to%20a%20market%2Dbased%20approach. Accessed 23 Aug 2022

Kane M (2022) China: plug-in car sales reached new monthly record in June 2022. InsideEVs. https://insideevs.com/news/601632/china-plugin-car-sales-june-2022/. Accessed 23 Aug 2022

NDRC (2022) China to further boost electric vehicle charging services. English. gov.cn. http://english.www.gov.cn/statecouncil/ministries/202201/22/content_WS61eb3b40c6d09c94e48a415d.html#:~:text=BEIJING%20%E2%80%94%20China%20will%20further%20boost,guideline%20published%20on%20Jan%2021. Accessed 23 Aug 2022

Wharton (2019) China's electric vehicle market: a storm of competition is coming. Knowledge at Wharton. https://knowledge.wharton.upenn.edu/article/chinas-ev-market/. Accessed 23 Aug 2022

Yang Z (2021) How China's quasi-carbon market for electric vehicles works. Protocol. https://www.protocol.com/china/dual-credit-policy. Accessed 23 Aug 2022

3

An Overview of the EV Stakeholders in China

Keywords Automakers • Traditional automakers • Joint ventures • Electric vehicle start-ups • Internet giants • Automotive suppliers • Mobility providers • Robotaxis • Ride-sharing

As the EV industry continues to grow at an exorbitant pace, the number of stakeholders looking to join the competition has also increased remarkably. Once content to wait on the sidelines, they are now all eyeing a slice of the increasingly large pie.

Notably, the attractive market is not the only thing encouraging more involvement from new parties. Previously, automakers only had to focus on one thing—making cars that could get from point A to point B. Nowadays, a car is much more than just a means of transportation; it has hundreds of components with much more advanced technology than ever before spanning several industries.

As the definition of what a car is becomes increasingly blurred, so do the lines between the different stakeholders. Nevertheless, it is practical to divide the different stakeholders in the EV industry into three categories: automakers, automotive suppliers, and mobility providers.

3.1   Automakers

In the highly competitive EV industry, Tesla has always been the one to beat. Its sharp rise to stardom, coupled with its continual technological advances, makes Tesla a formidable industry leader—but for how much longer?

In its shadow, admirers have been quietly working to overtake this industry giant. Chinese automakers are selling more EVs per hour than established Western automakers, and one, BYD, has achieved the highest EV sales of any company in the world. Just who are BYD and these other domestically dominant companies, and what impact are they having on international markets?

China's EV landscape is blossoming. While traditional Chinese automakers still dominate the market, growing EV start-ups with the backing of Internet giants are catching up and challenging their commanding position in the Chinese EV landscape. At the same time, as the market opens up, prominent Western automakers are also seeking to cooperate with domestic manufacturers, either through joint ventures established in recent years or by injecting new momentum into existing ones.

As seen in Figs. 3.1 and 3.2 (Chinese Automobile Dealers' Association 2021), there is a clear visible difference between the automakers that excel at selling traditional passenger vehicles and those that excel at selling EVs. The leading names in both charts have very few similarities,

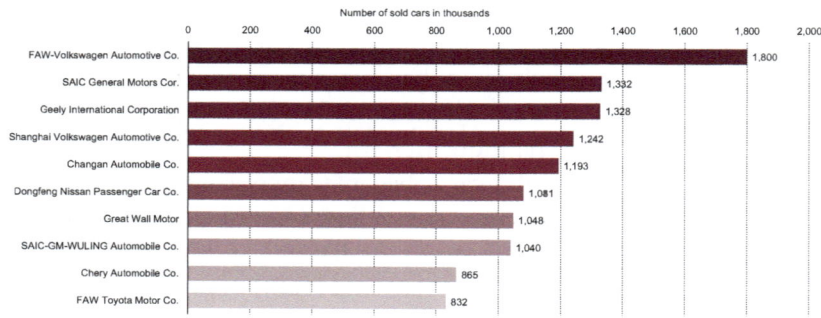

Fig. 3.1   Leading automakers based on number of vehicles sold in China in 2021 (Chinese Automobile Dealers' Association 2021)

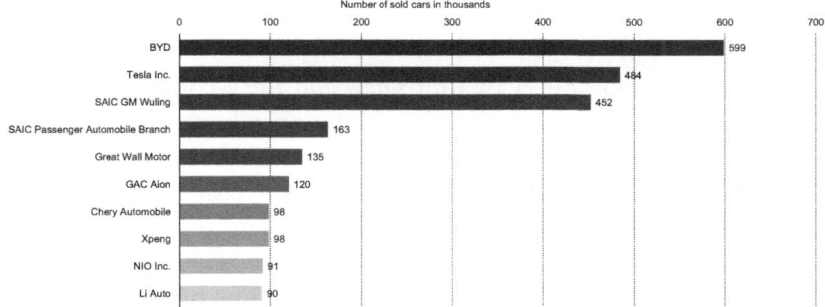

Fig. 3.2 Leading automakers based on number of EVs sold in China in 2021 (Chinese Automobile Dealers' Association 2021)

as it takes a whole different skillset to reach the top of each respective category. To gain a better understanding of the competition landscape, it is best to divide Chinese automakers into three subcategories:

1. Traditional automakers
2. Joint ventures between prominent Western and Chinese automakers
3. EV start-ups

3.1.1 Traditional Automakers

Traditional Chinese automakers currently dominate the domestic market. They are the leaders in terms of market share among all vehicle manufacturers and manufacturers of EVs. This is a result of their large production capacities and budgets, which allow them to target different market segments. They benefit from a long-standing supply chain as well as their brand name.

Traditional Chinese automakers are not widely known abroad but claim a dominant position in the domestic market and tend to have huge portfolios to meet the various demands of their base customers. The "Big Four" among domestic automakers are SAIC Motor, Dongfeng, FAW, and Changan, but in light of the rise of the EV industry, other traditional automakers have started stepping into the spotlight.

BYD

China's largest EV producer by unit sales, and the second largest in the world, also happens to be the world's leading producer of rechargeable batteries. In the first half of 2022, BYD surpassed Tesla in sales of plug-in EVs (BEVs and PHEVs) and is now closing in on Tesla in the BEV-only category as well, with its market share having doubled compared to the previous year (Kane 2022a).

BYD is committed to designing and manufacturing only pure-electric, zero-emissions cars in the near future and is gradually ceasing development and production of PHEVs. Their strongest advantage lies in their batteries. BYD has fully independent research and development (R&D), design, and production capacity. Having initially started off as a battery manufacturer that only later entered the automotive industry, their expertise serves them well in the EV market, where batteries are arguably the most important component of the vehicle.

BYD is also beginning to move into the international market. The company launched their Tang SUV in Norway in August 2021. By December 2021, BYD had sold 1000 vehicles, marking a successful entry into Europe (Automotive World 2021). They also plan to launch their EVs in Japan in 2023 (Randall 2022a).

Geely

Geely is a Chinese multinational automotive company headquartered in Hangzhou, Zhejiang. Founded in 1997, they were the third-largest automaker in China based on unit sales in 2021, having sold over 1.3 million vehicles.

In November 2021, Geely announced their "Smart Geely 2025" strategy. This demonstrates their commitment to smartification, as they aim to boost their sales and stake their claim as a world leader in the automotive industry. At the center of this strategy is the launch of their "Leishen Power" brand, an intelligent powertrain solutions provider. Alongside "Leishen Power" as part of their commitment to e-mobility, Geely will establish a "Smart Geely Technology Ecological Network" to build a future core competency around intelligent architectures, drive, and cockpits (Geely Auto 2021).

Within the European market, Geely has an advantage that most other Chinese automakers may envy. There may not be any Geely-branded cars on the road in Europe, but Volvo, Polestar, and Lotus are all part of its brand portfolio. Polestar has been well received worldwide. Its sales increased by 185% between 2020 and 2021, with the highest percentage of sales coming from Europe (Automotive News Europe 2022). This represents a promising start for Polestar (and for Geely), which has pledged to be fully electric by 2030. Through their mergers and acquisitions, they have circumvented one of the key issues that have hampered Chinese automakers in their attempts to enter international markets—a lack of confidence in a Chinese brand, that historically is not renowned for high quality.

> "We also believe that the future of the automotive industry is one that is built upon shared synergies and cross-industry partnerships. In this new era of ultimate disruption, no automotive brand can afford to go it alone, we must look to co-innovation of technologies, sharing of information and pooling resources to create a sustainable future."
>
> *- Geely CEO Daniel Li*

Changan

The automaker Changan traces its origins back to the Westernization movement that took place toward the end of the Qing dynasty. In November 1862, the Chinese politician, general, and diplomat Li Hongzhang founded the country's first Western-style engineering firm. From these humble beginnings, the company would evolve into Changan and launch its first production vehicle in 1959 on the 10th anniversary of the People's Republic of China. Today, it is the oldest automaker in China and was ranked fifth in terms of unit sales in 2021 (Changan Auto 2022).

At the 2021 Changan Auto Tech Ecosystem Summit, Changan announced their "New Auto, New Ecosystem" development strategy, with the goal of selling three million units in 2025, of which EVs would account for 35%. By 2030, Changan aims to have sales of 4.5 million units, with EVs accounting for 60% and international sales accounting for 30%, as a result of its efforts to become a world-class brand (DanZig 2022).

Similarly to Geely, Changan sees value in joint ventures and partnerships with other players in the automotive industry. In November 2021, they teamed up with the suppliers Huawei and CATL to produce the Avatr 11 EV (Shen 2021). Having recognized that their strengths lay elsewhere, they sought the assistance of other companies with autonomous driving and battery technology. Prior to this joint venture, they had also worked with BYD to produce batteries for their vehicles (BYD 2018).

3.1.2 Joint Ventures Between Western and Chinese Automakers

The trend for global automotive companies to increase investment in NEVs in China is unmistakable. Some companies decided to increase their cooperation with existing partners in order to compete in the dynamic market, while others chose to set up new joint ventures so that they are better prepared for the challenges posed by the fierce market competition.

Joint ventures between Chinese and Western automakers are not a new phenomenon, and they play a leading role in the general automotive market. Volkswagen and Nissan entered the Chinese market long ago, staking their claim based on their superior ICE vehicles. However, they are late to enter the race for EV market share. In fact, to even get started on gaining ground in the Chinese market, Western automakers must form joint ventures with local partners. Where such ventures exist, the partners mainly collaborate in development and production, targeting premium compact electrified vehicles.

SAIC-Volkswagen, FAW-Volkswagen, JAC-Volkswagen

The Volkswagen Group (VW) established its first joint venture in China with SAIC in 1984. After that, they began a joint venture with FAW in 1991. Their most recent joint venture was launched in 2017 with JAC. Volkswagen carries out their production, sales, and services in China through these joint ventures.

Europe's leading automaker has no issues selling its EVs at home. However, it is struggling to live up to its targets in China. In 2021, the company only sold 70,625 EVs on the Chinese market, a figure over-shadowed by Chinese EV start-ups NIO, XPeng, and Li Auto, which each sold between 90,000 and 100,000 EVs.

It is clear that VW has failed to establish the brand loyalty it hoped for among its potential Chinese consumers. New energy vehicles from Chinese manufacturers offer unique advanced technological features that are not found in competing Western models. This is arguably because Western customers see EVs more as vehicles with a different powertrain than what is traditional, as opposed to Chinese customers, who view EVs as smart terminals on wheels.

SAIC-GM-Wuling

SAIC-GM-Wuling (SGMW) is a joint venture between Chinese auto-makers Wuling and SAIC and American automaker General Motors. Formed in 2002, the joint venture has enjoyed great success, as the EV industry has boomed in recent years.

They manufacture the Wuling Hongguang Mini, the second-best-selling EV in 2021 (Kane 2022b), behind only the Tesla Model 3. This impressive sales total was achieved even though the model was only sold in China. The cost-effective parts used to make the Mini model enable the car to be priced at a low amount—approximately EUR 4750. Though the parts are less durable, they are easy to replace, making it a popular choice among consumers. Another reason why they can sell their EVs for such a low price is their control over the supply chain.

Now in 2022, SGMW is beginning to make their way overseas, first to Southeast Asia, with plans for the Wuling Hongguang Mini to be assembled and produced in Indonesia (Zhang 2022a). They plan to further strengthen their position through their "Two 'Million', Five 'Billion'" strategy, as part of which they plan to sell one million full-electric and hybrid vehicles in 2023 and expand their capabilities in five billion-dollar industries: batteries, electric drives, electronic control, business services, and robots (Sina 2022).

Dongfeng Nissan

Dongfeng Motor Company Limited, the Chinese joint venture of Dongfeng and Nissan, in which each company holds a 50% stake, was being referred to as "the biggest Sino–foreign vehicle joint venture" as of 2006 (China Daily 2006).

In 2018, the joint venture announced the introduction of a "green roadmap," which includes production and sales targets as well as the use of energy-saving production processes and second-life applications for used batteries. The company also plans to introduce at least 17 electrified models of the Dongfeng, Nissan, Venucia, and Infiniti brands by 2023 (Randall 2022b).

Sylphy Zero Emission, the first electric Nissan series model on the Chinese market, is the result of the cooperation between Nissan and Dongfeng and its electrification blueprint. The company started production of the EV in August 2018 and as Nissan's first BEV built in China specifically for Chinese consumers, the Nissan Sylphy Zero Emission promises to usher in a new era of electrification in the world's largest automotive market. The model was developed based on the platform of the world's best-selling EV, the Nissan LEAF, and the best-selling Nissan sedan in China, the Sylphy (Ren 2018).

3.1.3 Chinese EV Start-Ups

It is not just large established Chinese automakers that are booming and challenging the Western automotive industry. Competition is also coming from Chinese EV start-ups, whose spirit of innovation is disrupting the sector. The result is that these start-ups are gaining ground on established Chinese automakers.

Most of the start-ups are backed by tech giants, have an Internet background, and tend to employ tech geeks over automotive veterans. Their affinity with tech giants allows these EV start-ups to offer more than just a means of transportation, while tech companies can realize their fantasy of the next generation of EVs. Many Chinese EV start-ups are challenging the Western automotive industry with lower prices (for the same or better quality), technological innovations, and unique value propositions.

The speed at which these Chinese EV companies have garnered success domestically cannot be simply ascribed to luck. EV start-ups are offering not just a means of transportation, but a solution driven by data and AI, which can also be applied to online gaming, video streaming, Internet shopping, social media, and many more things. On the other hand, they tend to have leaner portfolios than traditional automakers and joint ventures, as their first aim is to validate how well their products fit the market.

NIO

NIO is a model example of Chinese NEV start-ups. Racing to outshine Tesla, NIO has gone from a start-up to one of China's top 10 EV brands in less than a decade. They have grown rapidly since their founding in 2014 and are now one of the biggest names associated with EVs.

In 2018, NIO filed for an initial public offering on the New York Stock Exchange, raising approximately EUR 1.8 billion (Franklin and Zhu 2018). Its advanced driver assistance system, known as NIO Pilot, is a direct competitor with Tesla's Autopilot. Its revolutionary concept of "battery as a service" (BaaS) has attracted vast attention. Customers can purchase NIO models without a battery, which makes NIO EVs considerably more affordable.

One thing that sets NIO apart from their competitors is their reimagination of the customer journey. With NIO House, the NIO App, and NIO Life, NIO offers their customers much more than just a vehicle, and they support their customers long after the initial purchase is made. They use this complete experience to differentiate themselves from their competitors and build customer loyalty. NIO made its European debut in Norway and aims to enter the wider European market from 2022 onward (Parikh 2022a), meaning it is clearly one to watch.

XPeng

Another rival for Tesla to contend with, the XPeng P7, is outselling the Tesla Model 3 in the Chinese market. XPeng's autonomous driving system "XPilot" is also set to rival Tesla's "Autopilot." With a successful launch in Norway already under their belt, this is yet another serious challenger (Parikh 2022b).

XPeng is taking a leaf out of Tesla's book when it comes to their sales and marketing strategies. All their sales are direct to customers, and the main selling point of their vehicles is their high-tech digital intelligence. Their vehicles only run Xmart OS, their own infotainment system, and are incompatible with others such as Apple CarPlay, and Android Auto. They have taken their first steps into the European market and hope that this will mark the beginning of their international expansion.

Their foray into Europe shows one way in which XPeng differentiates themselves from Tesla's strategy—through their aftersales services. After seeing how Tesla has struggled to provide suitable aftersales services to their customers due to their completely vertically integrated model, XPeng decided to partner with established dealer groups such as Emil Frey in the Netherlands to offer services. XPeng has also decided not to install their own network of chargers in Europe and instead has chosen to target European countries that already have a developed network of charging infrastructure, such as the Netherlands. This is in stark contrast to NIO, which has decided to build a network of battery-swapping stations. For XPeng, saving costs is a key goal, as they seek to make their first profits.

Li Auto

Li Auto is another of the many Chinese EV start-ups that are rapidly making their mark on China's NEV market. The company designs, develops, manufactures, and sells premium intelligent EVs. Their sales figures were only marginally behind those of start-up rivals NIO and XPeng in 2021 (Zhang 2022b).

So far in 2022, they have outperformed rivals Tesla, NIO, and XPeng on the stock market and intend to raise approximately EUR 2 billion through a stock offering to further fund research and development for their vehicles (Song 2022). As of August 2022, Li Auto has not entered any overseas markets yet, as they "aim to figure out how to win before we enter the war, rather than enter the war and then try to figure out how to survive" (Bloomberg 2022). However, there have been reports that they are considering opening a production site in Europe (Ren 2021).

3.2   Automotive Suppliers

Suppliers looking to secure their business for the long term are no longer content just supplying parts to automakers. They recognize the potential behind both EVs and autonomous driving, and as such, are leveraging their resources to play a bigger role in the development of these technologies. Automotive suppliers have started to team up with automakers to accelerate development by means of in-depth cooperation or even joint ventures.

A supplier like CATL wields a lot of power in the EV industry. They supply a third of the world's BEV battery capacity and approximately half of China's (Adham 2022). Because of their huge influence, they can strike more favorable deals, and automakers are willing to partner with them to secure their supply of batteries. What is more, they are not content with staying within China and are starting to expand overseas. They have built their first plant outside China in Arnstadt, Germany, and have plans to build another plant in the USA in an attempt to stay ahead of their competitors (Steitz and Klayman 2022).

Furthermore, a larger wave of capital has flowed from Internet giants to EV producers in recent years. New partnerships and business models are emerging, such as Internet giants Baidu and Tencent's investment in NIO, Alibaba's investment in XPeng, and other Internet giants' continuous investment in automotive infotainment systems, autonomous driving projects, and intelligent vehicle operating systems. All these innovations contribute to the general trend toward intelligent and interconnected EVs that provide revolutionary solutions for EV drivers.

An example of this is the launch of the Avita E11, a new intelligent EV developed by Changan, Huawei, and CATL. Together, they developed the CHN smart EV platform, which is equipped with Huawei's intelligent cockpit platform CDC, autonomous driving domain controller ADC, and some components of electric drive, batteries, and electric control (Sarkar 2022). SAIC and Alibaba have also come together in a joint venture to develop their own EV brand, known as IM Motors. This will adopt Alibaba's Banma Telematics system as well as SAIC's electric drive, battery, electric control, and intelligent driving technologies (Ackroyd 2022). Geely and Baidu have also started their own EV company called Jidu Auto, in which Baidu supplies the vehicles with their technologies, including artificial intelligence (AI), autonomous driving, Apollo, and Baidu Map, while Geely provides their automaking expertise (Liu and Ren 2021).

Huawei, Alibaba, and Baidu are nothing like traditional automotive suppliers. They are Internet behemoths—some of the biggest companies not just in China, but in the world. For them, the automotive industry represents just a fraction of their business. They are not reliant on Original Equipment Manufacturer (OEMs) in the same way that traditional suppliers typically are. As a result, they are not interested in simply taking directions from the automakers they work with. Instead, they aim to work together with these manufacturers as equals to create their vision of the car of the future. These players dare to challenge automakers in some cases and change the direction they take in developing and manufacturing cars.

Emerging Tier 1 suppliers, represented by Huawei and Mobileye, directly cooperate with automakers, participate heavily in product research and development, and position themselves as Tier 0.5 suppliers instead. Tier 0.5 suppliers fall somewhere between Tier 1 suppliers and automakers. While they do not manufacture cars themselves, they are more involved in the process than typical suppliers. Instead of just selling parts to automakers, Tier 0.5 suppliers are responsible for major systems and modules within the car, often collaborating directly and sharing information.

As an example, when BAIC's subsidiary Arcfox launched its R&D department, Huawei directly participated in research and development for the many system functions within the vehicle, including autonomous driving, intelligent cockpits, and smart electronics. Similarly, Mobileye acted as a Tier 0.5 supplier during their cooperation with Geely Lynk & Co. While Mobileye had only supplied semi-finished components to Tier 1 suppliers previously, it is now responsible for many different components, including hardware, software, drive strategy, and control.

Automotive suppliers in the EV industry are concerned with much more than just the components of individual vehicles. They are also responsible for charging stations, for example. Shell, one of the world's biggest oil and gas suppliers, recently announced plans to form a joint venture with BYD. The initial plan is to build more than 10,000 charging stations in Shenzhen, China, before expanding to other locations. Shell will also offer BYD's customers access to their extensive network of existing charging stations. As the EV industry continues to grow, other suppliers will likely develop a similar interest in charging infrastructure.

They may also become interested in BaaS, the battery-swapping solution pioneered by NIO as mentioned in Sect. 1.2. CATL, which supplies the batteries for many EV producers, including the market leader Tesla, announced in January 2022 that they would be launching their own innovative modular battery-swapping solution, EVOGO (CATL 2022). Thanks to CATL's unique expertise and position as the leading supplier of EV batteries, EVOGO will be compatible with 80% of battery-powered EVs available on the market for at least the next 3 years. CATL owes this broad compatibility to Choco-SEBs (swapping electric blocks), which work across many different classes of vehicles.

Oil giant BP has also acknowledged the potential behind battery-swapping solutions. It was already involved in the EV charging market through bp pulse, and in late 2021 it acquired a stake in Chinese battery-swapping specialist Aulton New Energy Automotive Technology Co., Ltd.. It plans to build even more battery-swapping stations within China, while also exploring the possibility of expanding abroad.

More and more suppliers are realizing that they can claim a bigger piece of the pie by getting more involved in the development of both intelligent and electric vehicles, as demonstrated by the many joint ventures mentioned above. The emergence of the Tier 0.5 cooperation model will reshape the cooperation pattern of the traditional automobile industry chain.

3.3   Mobility Providers

An often-overlooked group of companies that may have a role to play in the future of the automotive industry is mobility providers. There have been a lot of mixed signals recently about the future of private car ownership. Before the COVID-19 pandemic, statistics suggested that it was on the decline, with some reports even predicting that car ownership would reduce by 80% by 2030 (Garfield 2017). However, private car ownership has since rebounded in the wake of the pandemic, and people are buying cars in large numbers once again (Furcher et al. 2021).

Nevertheless, the need to travel (especially for work) has fallen over the course of the COVID-19 pandemic. Combined with a desire to cut the number of cars on the road so as to reduce pollution, this has prompted governments to invest more in public transportation. In China, the 14th five-year plan (2021–2025) is expected to extend the country's railways from 146,000–165,000 km and its subway lines from 6600 to 10,000 km. In the EU, the European Commission announced EUR 5.4 billion of investment in sustainable, safe, and efficient transportation infrastructure in June 2022, particularly aimed at making the rail network smarter and compatible across national borders (European Commission 2022). In the USA, the US Infrastructure Bill was passed in November 2021 and earmarks USD 112.5 billion for public transportation, over half of which will be put toward reforming rail services (Khara 2022).

As this expansion of public transportation systems continues, mobility providers will have an increasingly large role to play. According to a report by AlliedMarketResearch (Jadhav et al. 2021), the ride-sharing market was valued at approximately EUR 58.42 billion in 2020 and is projected to reach about EUR 201.98 billion by 2030, producing a CAGR of 13.2% from 2021 to 2030. Uber and Lyft have established widespread name recognition, but there are a considerable number of other companies that have entered or are seeking to enter the market. In China, one name stands apart from the rest as the undisputed market leader—Didi Chuxing.

With a market share of close to 90% (Global Times 2021), Didi Chuxing at one time practically dominated nationwide, though competition has risen locally on occasion, as other players try to claim some of their market share. Furthermore, Didi Chuxing has run into trouble with the Chinese government, further weakening their position.

Nonetheless, they are another stakeholder within the Chinese automotive industry that has decided to enter the EV market. In late 2020, they announced the D1, the world's first ride-sharing EV. The D1 was developed together with BYD, one the world's foremost EV producers. There were also reports in 2022 detailing their intention to continue producing EVs (The Business Times 2022; Zhang 2022c), as they stake a larger claim in the market.

An alternative to ride-sharing that is gaining steam in China is robotaxis. Using autonomous driving technology, customers can use robotaxis to go where they need to go without a driver on board. The global robotaxi market is expected to grow at a CAGR of 67.87% from 2023 to 2030 and is projected to reach approximately EUR 37.94 billion by 2030. There are many companies in China looking to capitalize on this opportunity, including automakers such as SAIC and Geely, which have formed partnerships with robotaxi market leaders to stake claims of their own.

Two of the robotaxi market leaders are Baidu, an Internet giant, and Pony.ai, a start-up that focuses on building autonomous driving solutions. Pony.ai is backed by Japanese automaker Toyota, and their software is used in Toyota cars. Meanwhile, Baidu operates their own brand of cars called Apollo. The development of robotaxis is progressing rapidly and Baidu obtained permits to operate fully driverless robotaxi services on open roads in August 2022, making it the first company to do so in China (Lo 2022). Mobility providers have already made their presence felt in the industry and will have a huge role to play in the years to come.

References

Ackroyd A (2022) Alibaba, SAIC venture start mass production of first electric vehicle. Alizila news from Alibaba. https://www.alizila.com/alibaba-saic-venture-start-mass-production-of-first-electric-vehicle/. Accessed 23 Aug 2022

Adham S (2022) H1 2022 battery and BEV production summary. LinkedIn https://www.linkedin.com/feed/update/urn:li:activity:69587809016735 94880/. Accessed 23 Aug 2022

Automotive News Europe (2022) How Polestar aims to reach breakeven next year, boosts sales tenfold by mid-decade. https://europe.autonews.com/automakers/how-polestar-aims-reach-breakeven-next-year-boost-sales-tenfold-mid-decade. Accessed 23 Aug 2022

Automotive World (2021) BYD delivers 1000th pure-electric Tang SUV in Norway. https://www.automotiveworld.com/news-releases/byd-delivers-1000th-pure-electric-tang-suv-in-norway/. Accessed 23 Aug 2022

Bloomberg (2022) Li Auto's heady EV sales target rests on winning over chipmakers. https://www.bloomberg.com/news/articles/2022-07-13/li-auto-s-heady-ev-sales-target-rests-on-winning-over-chipmakers. Accessed 23 Aug 2022

BYD (2018) BYD and Changan automobile launch groundbreaking battery joint venture. https://bydeurope.com/article/256. Accessed 23 Aug 2022

CATL (2022) CATL launches battery swap solution EVOGO featuring modular battery swapping. https://www.catl.com/en/news/856.html. Accessed 23 Aug 2022

Changan Auto (2022) One minute to understand Changan. http://www.global-changan.com/about_us/#:~:text=The%20Changan%20group%20dates%20back,what%20has%20become%20Changan%20Automobile. Accessed 23 Aug 2022

China Daily (2006) Dongfeng motor co relocates HQ to Wuhan. Chinaorgcn. http://www.china.org.cn/english/BAT/172445.htm. Accessed 23 Aug 2022

Chinese Automobile Dealers Association (2021) 2021年12月份全国乘用车市场深度分析报告 (national passenger car market in-depth analysis report for December 2021). CADAcn. http://www.cada.cn/xinche/info_118_8903.html. Accessed 23 Aug 2022

DanZig (2022) Changan automobile released the navy brand, with a sales target of 5.5 million units in 2030. LaiTimes. https://www.laitimes.com/en/article/3k7fh_40wg9.html. Accessed 23 Aug 2022

European Commission (2022) EU invests €5.4 billion in sustainable, safe, and efficient transport infrastructure. https://transport.ec.europa.eu/news/eu-invests-eu54-billion-sustainable-safe-and-efficient-transport-infrastructure-2022-06-29_en. Accessed 23 August 2022

Franklin J, Zhu J (2018) In Tesla's shadow, China's NIO raises $1 billion from IPO: sources. Reuters. https://www.reuters.com/article/us-nio-inc-ipo-idUSKCN1LR2QJ. Accessed 23 Aug 2022

Furcher T et al (2021) Car buying is on again, and mobility is picking up. McKinsey & Company. https://www.mckinsey.com/business-functions/growth-marketing-and-sales/our-insights/how-consumers-behavior-in-car-buying-and-mobility-changes-amid-covid-19. Accessed 23 Aug 2022

Garfield L (2017) Only 20% of Americans will own a car in 15 years, new study finds. Insider. https://www.businessinsider.com/no-one-will-own-a-car-in-the-future-2017-5. Accessed 23 Aug 2022

Geely Auto (2021) Geely auto group unveils smart Geely 2025 strategy. Geely Global Media Center. http://global.geely.com/media-center/news/geely-auto-group-unveils-smart-geely-2025-strategy/. Accessed 23 Aug 2022

Global Times (2021) Ride-hailing giants jostle for market share. https://www.globaltimes.cn/page/202107/1229125.shtml. Accessed 23 Aug 2022

Jadhav A et al (2021) Ride sharing market by booking type (online booking and offline booking), commute type (intracity and intercity), and vehicle type (cars, motorcycles, and others): global opportunity analysis and industry forecast, 2021–2030. All Market Res. https://www.alliedmarketresearch.com/ride-sharing-market-A13712#:~:text=The%20global%20ride%20sharing%20market,13.2%25%20from%202021%20to%202030. Accessed 23 Aug 2022

Kane M (2022a) World's top 5 EV automotive groups ranked by sales: H1 2022. InsideEVs. https://insideevs.com/news/601770/world-top-oem-ev-sales-2022h1/. Accessed 23 Aug 2022

Kane M (2022b) China: Wuling Hong Guang MINI EV sets massive sales record. InsideEVs. https://insideevs.com/news/560897/china-wuling-hongguang-sales-2021/. Accessed 23 Aug 2022

Khara I (2022) A massive step but is it enough? US Infrastructure Bill invests over $100 billion in public transport. UITP. https://www.uitp.org/news/a-massive-step-but-is-it-enough-us-infrastructure-bill-invests-over-100-billion-inpublic-transport/. Accessed 23 August 2022

Liu P, Ren D (2021) Chinese tech titan Baidu and carmaking giant Geely to pour US$7.7 billion into making next-generation smart cars. South China Morning Post. https://www.scmp.com/business/companies/article/3130852/chinese-tech-titan-baidu-and-carmaking-giant-geely-pour-us77. Accessed 23 Aug 2022

Lo F (2022) Baidu bags China's first fully driverless robotaxi licenses. Reuters. https://www.reuters.com/business/autos-transportation/baidu-bags-chinas-first-fully-driverless-robotaxi-licenses-2022-08-08/. Accessed 23 Aug 2022

Parikh S (2022a) Nio ES8 launched in Norway, ET7 & ET5 to follow. Topelectricsuv. https://topelectricsuv.com/news/nio/nio-overseas-launch-plan/. Accessed 23 Aug 2022

Parikh S (2022b) XPeng G3i (G3 facelift) launched in Norway. Topelectricsuv. https://topelectricsuv.com/news/xpeng/xpeng-g3-norway-global-launch/. Accessed 23 Aug 2022

Randall C (2022a) BYD plans to hit the Japanese market with 3 BEVs. Electrive. https://www.electrive.com/2022/07/22/byd-plans-to-hit-the-japanese-market-with-3-bevs/. Accessed 23 Aug 2022

Randall C (2022b) Nissan & Dongfeng announce 17 EVs by 2023. Electrive. https://www.electrive.com/2020/11/23/dongfeng-limited-announces-17-evs-by-2023/. Accessed 23 Aug 2022

Ren D (2021) Li Auto is mulling an overseas assembly to outgrow China's bare-knuckle market of electric vehicles. South China Morning Post. https://www.scmp.com/business/companies/article/3144656/li-auto-mulling-overseas-assembly-outgrow-chinas-bare-knuckle. Accessed 23 Aug 2022

Ren Q (2018) Dongfeng Nissan begins production of Sylphy zero emission electric car. Nissan Motor Corporation Official Global Newsroom. https://global.nissannews.com/en/releases/release-ed7b0014763a42e1693c5c954e1b7e81-180827-01-e. Accessed 23 Aug 2022

Sarkar A (2022) Huawei, CATL and Changan automobile's AVITA 11 smart car's details released. Huawaicentral.com https://www.huaweicentral.com/huawei-catl-and-changan-automobiles-avita-11-smart-cars-details-released/. Accessed 23 Aug 2022

Shen J (2021) Huawei debuts electric vehicle brand Avatr in tie-up with Changan, CATL. Technode. https://technode.com/2021/11/16/huawei-debuts-electric-vehicle-brand-avatr-suv-tie-up-with-changan-catl/. Accessed 23 Aug 2022

Sina (2022) 五菱新能源战略:2023年力争新能源汽车年销量达百万辆 (Wuling's new energy strategy: strive for annual sales of one million new energy vehicles in 2023) Finance.sina. https://finance.sina.com.cn/tech/2022-03-09/doc-imcwipih7451530.shtml. Accessed 23 Aug 2022

Song A (2022) Li Auto makes hay while electric sun shines. Reuters. https://www.reuters.com/breakingviews/li-auto-makes-hay-while-electric-sun-shines-2022-06-30/. Accessed 23 Aug 2022

Steitz C, Klayman B (2022) CATL planning EV battery production in United States, vetting sites. Reuters. https://www.reuters.com/technology/exclusive-catl-planning-ev-battery-production-united-states-vetting-sites-2022-05-06/. Accessed 23 Aug 2022

The Business Times (2022) Didi in talks with Haima Automobile about EV partnership: sources. https://www.businesstimes.com.sg/garage/didi-in-talks-with-haima-automobile-about-ev-partnership-sources. Accessed 23 Aug 2022

Zhang P (2022a) SAIC-GM-Wuling to assemble its mini EVs in Indonesia. CnEVPost. https://cnevpost.com/2022/05/26/saic-gm-wuling-to-assemble-its-mini-evs-in-indonesia/. Accessed 23 Aug 2022

Zhang P (2022b) Deliveries: how does NIO compare to XPeng and Li Auto? CnEVPost. https://cnevpost.com/2022/01/01/deliveries-how-does-nio-compare-to-xpeng-and-li-auto/. Accessed 11 Oct 2022

Zhang P (2022c) Didi reportedly could announce car-making plans in June. CnEVPost. https://cnevpost.com/2022/03/15/didi-reportedly-could-announce-car-making-plans-in-june/. Accessed 23 Aug 2022

4

Electrification: Routes to the Future

Keywords Electric vehicle powertrains • Range anxiety • Charging infrastructure • Battery swapping • Battery-as-a-service • Battery supply chain • Battery value chain

The blossoming of the EV industry is also presenting a new set of challenges related to powering the cars themselves. There are two key factors in how an electric vehicle operates—the battery and the charging infrastructure.

For the EV industry to prosper, both the battery and the charging infrastructure have to advance in tandem. China seems to be well ahead of other countries in this respect. This chapter will further explore how China is moving forward and overcoming obstacles that have been prevalent in the EV industry for years.

4.1 EV Powertrains

So far, this book has largely referred to BEVs and PHEVs simply as EVs, but it is worth remembering that this is an umbrella term. There are more ways of classifying EVs than just into those two categories. Categorizing

J. Y. Yang et al., *Chinese Electric Vehicle Trailblazers*, Business Guides on the Go,
https://doi.org/10.1007/978-3-031-25145-0_4

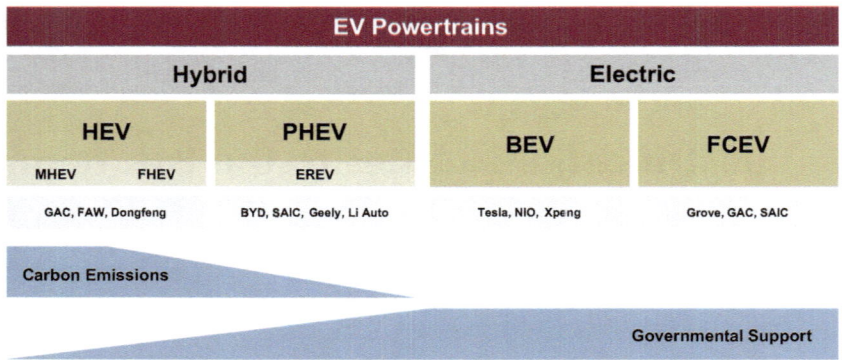

Fig. 4.1 Breakdown of EV powertrains

vehicles appropriately is highly important, as each category of EV requires specific expertise to manufacture and is best suited to a particular market segment. The main categories are battery electric vehicles (BEVs), plug-in hybrid electric vehicles (PHEVs), hybrid electric vehicles (HEVs), and fuel cell electric vehicles (FCEVs), summarized in Fig. 4.1.

Battery Electric Vehicles (BEVs)

BEVs are completely powered by electricity. This means they have no ICE, no fuel tank, and no exhaust pipe. As the world moves toward electrification, these features are seen as the future of the automotive industry. The main benefits of BEVs over ICE vehicles are that the electricity they need costs less than gasoline, and they are environmentally friendly since they produce substantially less emissions.

However, the drawbacks include a higher up-front cost due to the battery and a lack of choice in the market compared to ICE vehicles, HEVs, and PHEVs. Furthermore, even though the ranges of BEVs are improving, the lack of charging infrastructure and long charging times cause range anxiety, a driver's fear that their vehicle will run out of power before they reach their destination. This may force them to wait to recharge their battery or leave them stranded miles from a charging station. BEV technology is constantly improving, and many of the existing drawbacks are being alleviated. The main BEV players currently include Tesla, NIO, and XPeng.

Plug-In Hybrid Electric Vehicles (PHEVs)

PHEVs are the halfway point between BEVs and HEVs. Similarly to BEVs, they have a battery that can be charged via an external plug. However, they also have an ICE. The PHEV aims to combine the best of both worlds. On shorter trips, only the electric motor is used, thus reducing emissions and fuel costs. On longer trips and in emergencies, the ICE is available as a back-up, keeping range anxiety at bay.

However, battery technology and charging infrastructure are improving and the range of BEVs will eventually match or even exceed that of PHEVs. At that point, the advantages of a PHEV will evaporate. Furthermore, since governments are pushing for greener alternatives, there are fewer subsidies available for PHEVs than for BEVs (ICC 2020), since they release emissions even under ideal conditions.

Another subset of PHEVs is extended-range electric vehicles (EREVs), which act as another intermediate step between PHEVs and BEVs. While EREVs still have an ICE within the car, it never directly propels the car. Instead, it generates electricity that can be supplied to the battery. Although EREVs have lost popularity in recent years with the rise of BEVs, Chinese EV start-up Li Auto has carved out a niche within the EV market by offering exclusively EREVs. Their latest model (Li L9) has a maximum range of 1315 km (817 miles) (Li Auto 2022).

Hybrid Electric Vehicles (HEVs)

HEVs are the most common type of hybrid vehicles. Like BEVS and PHEVs, they have an electric motor. However, the battery cannot be charged with an external plug—instead, the battery is charged through a process known as regenerative braking, in which the kinetic energy from braking is captured and converted into electrical energy to charge the car's battery. This is done using supercapacitors, an alternative to storing electrical energy. Supercapacitors charge and discharge electrical energy quickly but cannot store much of it, making them suitable for this application.

The benefits of HEVs are that they are more fuel-efficient than pure ICE vehicles, as the stored energy from regenerative braking is used to power the car. However, they still predominantly rely on ICEs, meaning they are not as environmentally friendly as PHEVs or BEVs.

HEVs can be further divided into full hybrid vehicles and mild hybrid vehicles. Full hybrids can use both the ICE and the electric motor to power the car. However, since the batteries are typically smaller compared to BEVs and PHEVs, the electric motor can only power the car for short distances and at lower speeds. Mild hybrids cannot be powered using only the electric motor. Instead, the electric motor simply assists the ICE, powering the car when idling and helping during acceleration.

Fuel Cell Electric Vehicles (FCEVs)

FCEVs use hydrogen as a source of fuel for chemical reactions to generate electricity. There is yet another green alternative to ICE vehicles. The benefits of hydrogen FCEVs over BEVs are their greater range and shorter refueling time. However, the FCEV market is still in its infancy compared to the general EV market, as doubts remain over the feasibility of hydrogen as a fuel source.

While the process of converting hydrogen to electricity is sound, generating hydrogen gas is the real problem. On the one hand, it is possible to generate hydrogen gas without producing carbon emissions through the process of electrolysis, but it is uncommon and expensive. On the other hand, 95% of the world's hydrogen gas today is generated using natural gas, which is cheaper but results in significant carbon dioxide emissions (Wyatt 2022).

The Chinese government is also taking steps to help the FCEV industry grow. In March 2022, the government revealed its latest policy blueprint for FCEVs, which aims to have 50,000 FCEVs on the road by 2025 (Li 2022). The government will encourage partnerships to foster innovation and make the technology more profitable. If the methods of producing hydrogen gas can be improved in the next few years, this could be an exciting alternative to BEVs.

4.2   Charging Infrastructure

The second key factor in the successful operation of EVs is the charging infrastructure. While organizations have varying definitions for fast and slow chargers, the IEA defines slow chargers as having a charge rate less than or equal to 22 kilowatts (kW), whereas fast chargers have a charge rate of more than 22 kW (IEA 2022a). China is expanding its network of charging stations (both fast and slow) and potentially adopting battery-swapping technology. With the support of the national government, more than 800,000 publicly available charging stations have been installed in China, a number far greater than in any other country in the world.

The sheer number of publicly available chargers built in China is merely part of the story. According to the IEA, China had among the highest EV to charger and kW of charging power per EV rates in the world in 2021. Meanwhile, the European Union and the rest of the world have fallen behind, as shown in Table 4.1 (IEA 2022a). Only a select few countries like South Korea and the Netherlands have better charging infrastructure than China when accounting for the difference in population.

Though it may seem as though China is just single-mindedly pursuing the highest possible number, the country is in fact adapting its charging infrastructure to better match and manage consumer demands. This will increase demand for EVs in the future and guarantee success for domestic automakers.

There are many reasons why China's charging infrastructure is so much more developed than the rest of the world. For example, the Chinese government has always insisted on interoperability for their charging infrastructure, meaning that all EVs and charging stations use the same plugs and outlets. Furthermore, payment systems for using charging stations throughout China are standardized, with WeChat Pay and AliPay being the most common (Conrad 2022).

Other examples of the Chinese government's efforts to speed up adoption of EVs by improving charging infrastructure include offering financial subsidies to companies that build charging infrastructure and encouraging banks to provide them with favorable policies (Zhang 2022).

Table 4.1 China's charging infrastructure in comparison to the rest of the world (IEA 2022a)

Country/region	EVs per charger	kW per EV
China	7	3.8
European Union	14	1.0
World	10	2.4

In January 2022, the government released a document (Chinese Development and Reform Commission 2022), which lists several concrete goals. One goal is that all newly built residential complexes must offer charging stations and all existing complexes must convert their parking spaces to allow EVs to be charged if possible. The document also stipulates that 60% of expressway service stations nationwide must be equipped with fast charging stations, rising to 80% in regions with high levels of air pollution.

4.3   Battery Supply Chain

The cost of batteries is lower in China than in any other country because most of the battery supply chain is domestic. Furthermore, China's supply chain is extremely well-developed due to the government's aggressive policies to promote local suppliers, such as requiring automakers to use batteries from an allowlist of domestic companies in order to be eligible for government subsidies (Yi 2019). This has led to the rise of domestic battery giants like BYD and CATL, whose respective market shares in 2021 are shown in Table 4.2 (Huang et al. 2021).

China produces three-quarters of all lithium-ion batteries and is home to 70% of the world's production capacity for cathodes and 85% for anodes. Both are key components of batteries. Over half of global lithium, cobalt, and graphite processing and refining capacity is also in China (IEA 2022b). The country has access to almost the entire battery value chain shown in Fig. 4.2 (Finnish Minerals Group 2022) within its borders, which gives it a commanding global position as the EV industry grows. The only resources that China lacks domestically are certain raw materials such as cobalt and nickel, though companies have been able to secure these from countries like the Democratic Republic of the Congo and Australia.

Nowadays, although governmental support for battery manufacturers is being phased out, the positive effects of that investment can still be seen. Chinese battery manufacturers like CATL and BYD have built up a wealth of expertise and invested in the whole supply chain, from

Table 4.2 Top 10 battery manufacturers in 2021 by market share (Randall 2022)

1	CATL		32.6%
2	LG Energy Solution		20.3%
3	Panasonic		12.2%
4	BYD		8.8%
5	SK On		5.6%
6	Samsung SDI		4.5%
7	CALB		2.7%
8	Gotion High-Tech		2.1%
9	AESC		1.4%
10	SVOLT		1.0%

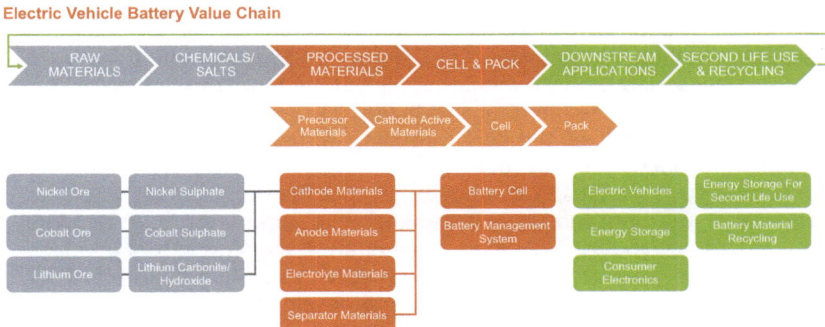

Fig. 4.2 Electric vehicle battery value chain (Finnish Minerals Group 2022)

mining and refining materials to manufacturing and even recycling battery cells (Meaker 2022). What follows is a case study of CATL, a company that has grown tremendously in recent years and plays a huge role in the EV industry today.

The Rise of CATL

As mentioned in Sect. 3.2, CATL is an automotive supplier in the EV industry that has enjoyed a meteoric rise to the top. Founded in 2011, CATL has benefitted from the Chinese government's support of the EV industry and is now the market leader in the battery industry, with 32.6% global market share in 2021. Within China, their market share is even greater at 52.1% (Zhang 2022a).

When CATL first started producing batteries, their competitor BYD was considered the market leader. However, CATL's nickel manganese cobalt (NMC) batteries provided cars with greater range than BYD's lithium iron phosphate batteries. The company was able to take advantage of this in 2015 when China rolled out further EV subsidies tied to range—EVs with longer ranges would be eligible for more generous subsidies. This was part of China's "Made in China 2025" plan. Another component was that customers who bought EVs would receive tax breaks, but only if the EVs included batteries made by Chinese manufacturers on the government's allowlist.

This tactic increased demand for Chinese batteries and fueled the growth of CATL. Buoyed by this, CATL continued to raise money by issuing shares and invested heavily in both their R&D and supply chain. Their investment in the latter allowed them to take control of the battery industry. The cost of EVs heavily depends on the upstream cost of batteries, and the cost of batteries in turn heavily depends on the upstream cost of their raw materials. CATL recognized this and therefore has acquired and continues to acquire several mining projects, both domestically and internationally, to secure their supply of raw materials. Some of their more recent investments include lithium mines in China (Mining 2022a), cobalt mines in the Democratic Republic of the Congo (Mining Technology 2021), and nickel mines in Indonesia (Mining 2022b).

Furthermore, they have leveraged their position as a market leader to form joint ventures and sign agreements with automakers such as SAIC, Geely, Daimler, and BMW. As a result, when the ban on using foreign-made batteries was repealed in 2019, CATL was able to maintain their lead. They continue to invest heavily in research and development to improve their batteries and maintain their competitive edge, as shown in Fig. 4.3 (Gasgoo 2022). All these factors have led to CATL becoming the foremost battery manufacturer in the world, with the company showing no signs of slowing down.

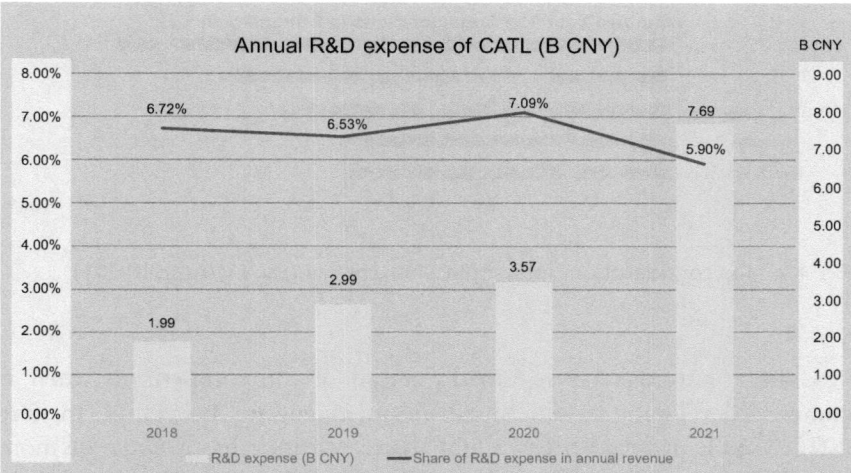

Fig. 4.3 CATL R&D expenditure in absolute terms and as a share of company revenue (Gasgoo 2022)

4.4 Range Anxiety

An EV's main value depends on the reliability, range, and quality of its battery. If any of those factors are compromised, drivers have to contend with range anxiety, the fear that their vehicle will run out of power before they reach their destination. This may force them to wait to recharge their battery or leave them stranded miles from a charging station. Range anxiety is also a common reason why consumers decide against purchasing an EV when looking to buy a new vehicle. Figure 4.4 (Autolist 2021) shows the results of a survey based on customer priorities when buying an EV, where 61% of people chose range as their top consideration when choosing an EV. This represents an increase of 18 percentage points over the previous survey done in 2019, overtaking price and charging infrastructure as the top consideration. Having recognized that range anxiety is the single biggest hurdle to overcome if they are going to increase EV sales, Chinese automakers are turning their attention toward increasing the range of their EVs.

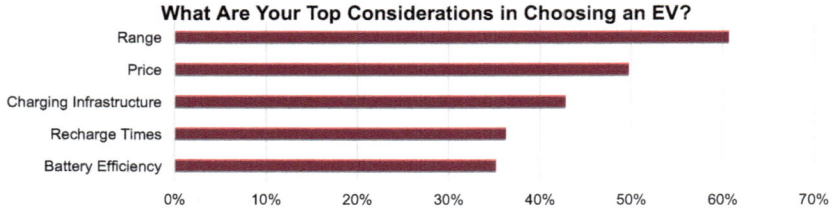

Fig. 4.4 Top considerations for people when choosing an EV (Autolist 2021)

Chinese automakers are broadly ahead of the competition when it comes to developing batteries for EVs and extending their range. In June 2022, CATL unveiled their "Qilin" battery, which has a range of more than 1000 km, and is safer and more durable than units that were already available. They are set to begin mass production in 2023, with EV start-ups Li Auto Inc. and Hozon New Energy Automobile Co. lined up as customers (Bloomberg 2022). With the same chemistry and size, Qilin can deliver 13% more power compared to Tesla's latest battery, the 4680. The Chinese automakers NIO (Hampel 2021) and GAC (Doll 2022) have also unveiled cars with a range of 1000 km, while Volkswagen lags behind with other competitors, offering ranges of just 700 km (Lambert 2022).

This speaks volumes as to how far the Chinese automotive industry has come. While Chinese ICE vehicles were always regarded as of low quality, China is now setting the benchmark in the EV industry. Their battery technology is the envy of the world, and their EVs can rival or even overshadow their international counterparts.

Nevertheless, range anxiety is often overblown. While a longer range is desirable in most cases, it is not always necessary, as shown in Fig. 4.5 (Gehring et al. 2022). The Simon-Kucher and Partners Global Automotive Study 2022 shows that the minimum range most people expect of an EV is below 600 km, with the average expected minimal range of 519 km.

Elon Musk has also questioned the necessity of long ranges for EVs, claiming that Tesla could manufacture cars with longer ranges, but chooses not to (Reuter 2022). This is backed up by the fact that the

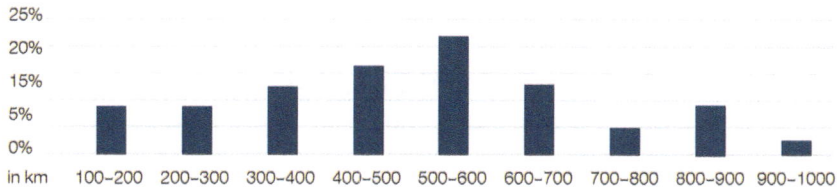

Fig. 4.5 Customers' expectations of minimum range of EVs (Gehring et al. 2022)

Wuling Hongguang Mini was the second best-selling EV in the world in 2021, with a total of 395,451 units sold (Kane 2021a), despite its maximum range of 170 km. This means the question for Chinese automakers is not whether they could manufacture cars with long ranges, but whether they should.

> "99.9% of time you'd be carrying unneeded battery mass, which makes acceleration, handling & efficiency worse."
>
> *- Tesla CEO Elon Musk*

4.5 Battery-Swapping Trend

While charging stations are currently the most widespread solution to powering an EV, Chinese automakers are exploring different ways of overcoming the issue of long charging times. Traffic at peak times often makes the process of charging even longer. While fast chargers alleviate this issue to a certain extent, there is still room for improvement. As mentioned in Sects. 1.2 and 3.2, Chinese EV start-up NIO introduced a new innovation to the problem of charging EVs by launching NIO BaaS in 2020 (NIO 2020), a battery-swapping solution.

BaaS has several benefits. Firstly, it is designed to alleviate range anxiety, as customers can swap their depleted batteries for fully charged ones in under 5 min. Furthermore, customers do not have to pay up front for the battery, which is a significant portion of an EV's price. Instead, they enjoy CNY 70,000 (about EUR 10,000) off the price of the car in exchange for a monthly subscription to the service. Lastly, customers can choose to opt in or out of BaaS and upgrade their battery to a better one when needed, giving them more flexibility. These benefits are all very attractive to customers, who may choose to buy EVs from NIO as a result.

Case Study: Better Place

The concept of battery swapping is not new. The first battery-swapping service was launched by General Electric in 1912, before being discontinued in 1924 due to waning demand. More recently, the Israeli company Better Place, founded in 2007, took on the challenge of bringing this service back to market, managing to raise approximately EUR 850 million (Carey and Lienert 2022). Its approach was very similar to NIO's; a depleted battery would be replaced with a fully charged one in 5 min at one of Better Place's battery-swapping stations. However, the company's efforts fell short, and it filed for bankruptcy in 2013. What went wrong for Better Place?

One issue they faced was a lack of support from the Israeli government. At the time, Israel provided no subsidies for EVs, and drivers had to pay usage tax that reflected the full value of the car, including the battery. Battery swapping is intended to save drivers the cost of owning the battery, so this tax status undermined the benefit that Better Place offered. This was just one of the ways the Israeli government put obstacles in the way of Better Place's growth.

Furthermore, adoption of EVs was not nearly as widespread as it is today, and automakers were skeptical of battery-swapping technology. In the end, Renault-Nissan was the only automaker willing to build vehicles compatible with Better Place. This was perhaps the most important reason behind the failure of Better Place, as it failed to get sufficient automakers on board. As a result, customers were not convinced either. They did not have many choices when it came to cars, and the battery-swapping stations were not widespread, with only 37 built in Israel.

In conclusion, the fault did not lie with the idea or technology. Better Place was ahead of its time, and the automotive industry was not ready yet for battery swapping. Nowadays, the EV industry is a lot more developed, with more support from governments and automakers. Customers are also warming up to EVs, especially in China, as the world moves toward electrification.

NIO is having considerably more success than predecessors using the same business model. NIO has already built more than 800 stations, with plans to build a total of 1300 stations by the end of 2022 (Zhang 2022b).

Other automakers such as Aulton New Energy Automotive Technology Co., Ltd. and Geely have also joined in, and the number of battery-swapping stations is set to massively increase in the years to come.

More and more companies are joining this trend. This is not limited to just automakers—suppliers also recognize it as a huge opportunity. These suppliers include CATL, which has entered the market with its own modular battery-swapping solution known as EVOGO, as mentioned in Sect. 3.2.

NIO's domestic success, shown in Fig. 4.6 (Kane 2021b), provides a potential blueprint for success in international markets. The company is now in talks to license its battery-swapping technology to some of its rivals, which could accelerate adoption in markets like Europe. A study undertaken by Astute Analytica in 2022 foresees the global BaaS market growing from approximately EUR 140 million in 2021 to approximately EUR 1.08 billion by the end of 2030, a CAGR of 25.9% (Astute Analytica 2022).

However, there are some concerns about the long-term feasibility of battery-swapping technology. As ranges and charging times of EVs steadily improve, some observers are beginning to fear that battery swapping may become obsolete. Tesla piloted the technology but abandoned it in 2021, claiming that battery swapping was riddled with problems and not suitable for large-scale use (Lomberg 2022). Furthermore, NIO itself bears a heavy financial burden by offering battery services. The cost

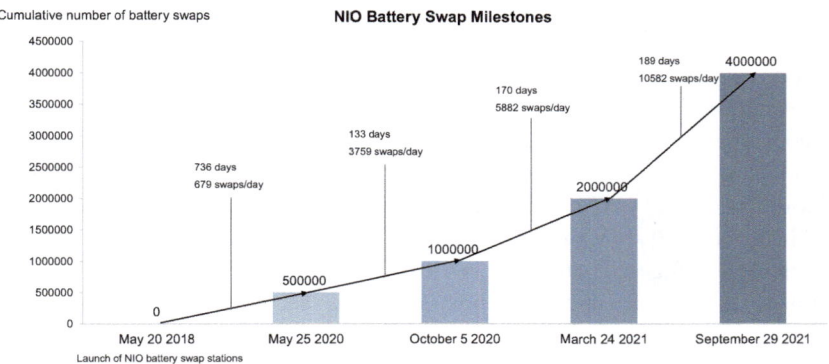

Fig. 4.6 Usage of NIO's battery-swapping service following adoption of their BaaS model (Kane 2021b)

of building battery-swapping stations (around EUR 500,000) and the batteries themselves are borne exclusively by NIO and not the customer. While their customers are pleased with the service and the convenience it provides, NIO has to pay for the electricity at commercial/industrial rates, which are far greater than residential rates. While BaaS has proven itself a popular choice for customers, the costs associated with it make it difficult for NIO to break even.

The failure of Better Place to kick off battery swapping is something to take note of and learn from, but so much has changed in the automotive industry since then. Though it still has its fair share of doubters, battery swapping is now in a much stronger position. In November 2021, the Ministry of Industry and Information Technology (MIIT) launched a battery-swapping pilot to further standardize battery swapping within China (Liu 2020). As mentioned earlier, other automakers are also implementing the technology, and CATL's support of battery-swapping technology could prove crucial, as they are the market leader among battery manufacturers and supply many automakers. Even if range gradually recedes as a concern, the flexibility offered to customers by battery swapping and BaaS will ensure it has a unique selling point.

References

Astute Analytica (2022) Battery as a service market—industry dynamics, market size, and opportunity forecast to 2030. https://www.astuteanalytica.com/industry-report/battery-as-a-service-market. Accessed 23 Aug 2022

Autolist (2021) Survey: electric vehicles' range jumps to top of priorities for consumers. https://www.autolist.com/news-and-analysis/2021-survey-electric-vehicles. Accessed 23 Aug 2022

Bloomberg (2022) CATL's 1000-kilometer range EV battery picked by Li Auto, Hozon. https://www.bloomberg.com/news/articles/2022-06-24/catl-s-1-000-kilometer-range-ev-battery-picked-by-li-auto-hozon. Accessed 23 Aug 2022

Carey N, Lienert P (2022) Factbox: swapping electric car batteries since the Gilded Age. https://www.reuters.com/business/aerospace-defense/swapping-electric-car-batteries-since-gilded-age-2022-03-24/. Accessed 20 Oct 2022

Chinese Development and Reform Commission (2022) 国家发展改革委等部门关于进一步提升电动汽车充电基础设施服务保障能力的实施意

见 (Implementation opinions of the national development and reform commission and other departments on further improving the service support capability of electric vehicle charging infrastructure). Govcn. http://www.gov.cn/zhengce/zhengceku/2022-01/21/content_5669780.htm. Accessed 23 Aug 2022

Conrad J (2022) China is racing to electrify its future. Wired. https://www.wired.com/story/china-ev-infrastructure-charging/. Accessed 23 Aug 2022

Doll S (2022) GAC Aion begins sales of LX plus SUV with 1,008 km (626 miles) NEDC range for just over $72,000. Electrek. https://electrek.co/2022/01/05/gac-aion-begins-sales-of-lx-plus-suv-with-1008-km-626-miles-nedc-range-for-just-over-72000/. Accessed 23 Aug 2022

Finnish Minerals Group (2022), Battery value chain. Finnish Minerals Group. https://www.mineralsgroup.fi/mission/battery-value-chain.html. Accessed 23 Aug 2022

Gasgoo (2022) Tesla becomes CATL's biggest client in 2021. Gasgoo China Automotive News. https://autonews.gasgoo.com/new_energy/70020168.html#:~:text=In%20addition%2C%20CATL's%20annual%20R%26D,of%20the%20company's%20total%20revenue. Accessed 23 Aug 2022

Gehring M et al (2022) Global automotive study 2022. Simon-Kucher & Partners. https://www.simon-kucher.com/sites/default/files/2022-02/Brochure_Automotive-Study-2022.pdf. Accessed 23 Aug 2022

Hampel C (2021) Nio reveals 1,000-km range sedan and EU plans. Electrive. https://www.electrive.com/2021/12/20/nio-reveals-new-mid-sized-sedan-and-eu-plans/#:~:text=Chinese%20EV%20manufacturer%20Nio%20has,Sweden%20and%20Denmark%20in%202022.%E2%80%9D. Accessed 23 Aug 2022

Huang Z et al (2021) China's electric vehicle battery industry: past, present and future. BatteryBits. https://medium.com/batterybits/chinas-electric-vehicle-battery-industry-past-present-and-future-937f9b061f5a. Accessed 23 Aug 2022

ICC (2020) China announced 2020–2022 subsidies for new energy vehicles. International Council on Clean Transportation. https://theicct.org/sites/default/files/publications/China%20NEV-policyupdate-jul2020.pdf. Accessed 23 Aug 2022

IEA (2022a) Trends in charging infrastructure: charging infrastructure is expanding significantly. Global EV Outlook 2022. https://www.iea.org/reports/global-ev-outlook-2022/trends-in-charging-infrastructure. Accessed 23 Aug 2022

IEA (2022b) Global supply chains of EV batteries. Global EV Outlook 2022. https://iea.blob.core.windows.net/assets/4eb8c252-76b1-4710-8f5e-867e75 1c8dda/GlobalSupplyChainsofEVBatteries.pdf. Accessed 23 Aug 2022

Kane M (2021a) China: Wuling Hong Guang MINI EV sets massive sales record. InsideEVs. https://insideevs.com/news/560897/china-wuling-hong guang-sales-2021/. Accessed 23 Aug 2022

Kane M (2021b) China: NIO reports 4 millionth EV battery swap. InsideEVs.. https://insideevs.com/news/537644/nio-4-million-battery-swaps/. Accessed 23 Aug 2022

Lambert, F (2022), VW is preparing some improvements to MEB electric vehicles, including range of up to 435 miles (700 km). Electrek. https://electrek. co/2022/04/13/vw-preparing-improvements-meb-electric-vehicles-range-435-miles-700-km/#:~:text=VW%20is%20preparing%20some%20 good,435%20miles%20(700%20km). Accessed 23 Aug 2022

Li Auto (2022) Li Auto Inc. Unveils Li L9, Its Flagship Smart SUV. Li Auto Press Release. https://ir.lixiang.com/news-releases/news-release-details/li-auto-inc-unveils-li-l9-its-flagship-smart-suv. Accessed 23 Aug 2022

Li F (2022) China sets out blueprint for fuel cell vehicles for 2025. China Daily. https://www.chinadaily.com.cn/a/202203/28/WS624117a2a310fd2b29 e53a40.html. Accessed 23 Aug 2022

Liu J (2020) 工信部:鼓励企业研发新型充电和换电技术 满足不同市场需要 (Ministry of Industry and Information Technology: encourage enterprises to develop new charging and power exchange technologies to meet the needs of different markets). Autopeoplecn. http://auto.people.com.cn/n1/2020/ 0723/c1005-31795218.html. Accessed 23 Aug 2022

Lomberg J (2022) Why did Tesla give up on battery swapping? Powersystemdesign. com. https://www.powersystemsdesign.com/articles/why-did-tesla-give-up-on-battery-swapping/131/18891#:~:text=And%20about%20a%20year%20 ago,not%20suitable%20for%20widescale%20use.%E2%80%9D. Accessed 23 Aug 2022

Meaker M (2022) The rise and precarious reign of China's battery king. Wired. https://www.wired.com/story/catl-china-battery-production-evs/. Accessed 23 Aug 2022

Mining (2022a) CATL wins $135m lithium project in race for materials. https://www.mining.com/catl-wins-135m-lithium-project-in-race-for-materials/#:~:text=China's%20Contemporary%20Amperex%20Techno logy%20(CATL,million%20yuan%20(%24134.76%20million). Accessed 23 Aug 2022

Mining (2022b) CATL joins $6 billion mining-to-batteries complex venture in Indonesia. https://www.mining.com/web/catl-joins-6-billion-venture-in-indonesia/. Accessed 23 Aug 2022

Mining Technology (2021) CATL to acquire stake in DRC's Kisanfu copper-cobalt mine in $137m deal. https://www.mining-technology.com/news/catl-acquire-stake-drcs-kisanfu-copper-cobalt-mine-137m-deal/. Accessed 23 Aug 2022

NIO (2020) NIO launches battery as a service. NIO Newsroom. https://www.nio.com/news/nio-launches-battery-service. Accessed 23 Aug 2022

Randall C (2022) CATL outgrows the battery competition. Electrive. https://www.electrive.com/2022/02/08/catl-outgrows-the-battery-competition/. Accessed 23 Aug 2022

Reuter D (2022) Elon Musk explains why Tesla hasn't tried to make the world's longest-range electric car: 'That would've made the product worse'. Insider. https://www.businessinsider.com/musk-explains-why-tesla-wont-make-longest-range-ev-2022-3#:~:text=Tesla%20won't%20be%20trying,most%20drivers%20won't%20use. Accessed 23 Aug 2022

Wyatt D (2022) Fuel cells are not the problem, the hydrogen fuel is. IDTechEx. https://www.idtechex.com/en/research-article/fuel-cells-are-not-the-problem-the-hydrogen-fuel-is/25913. Accessed 23 Aug 2022

Yi J (2019) China's "White list" of power battery companies abolished. Neware battery testing system expert. https://newarebattery.com/chinas-white-list-of-power-battery-companies-abolished/. Accessed 23 Aug 2022

Zhang, P (2022a) CATL dominates China EV battery market with 52.1% share in 2021. CnEVPost. https://cnevpost.com/2022/01/13/catl-dominates-china-ev-battery-market-with-52-1-share-in-2021/. Accessed 23 Aug 2022

Zhang P (2022b) NIO aims to have over 1,300 swap stations in China by end of 2022. CnEVPost. https://cnevpost.com/2021/12/19/nio-aims-to-have-1300-swap-stations-in-china-by-end-of-2022/. Accessed 23 Aug 2022

Zhang Z (2022) China plans charging infrastructure for 20 million EVs. Protocol. https://www.protocol.com/bulletins/china-infrastructure-plan-ev. Accessed 23 Aug 2022

5

Smartification: The Holy Grail of EV

Keywords Smartification • Electric vehicle intelligence • Intelligent cockpit • Internet of vehicles • Autonomous driving • V2X (vehicle to everything)

Why is Tesla so successful? There are many answers to this question, such as its early entry into the burgeoning industry and its ability to anticipate demand. However, one big reason for Tesla's success is the intelligence of its vehicles. Elon Musk himself has made the claim that Tesla is increasingly becoming an AI and robotics company (Lambert 2021), which is a testament to how deeply interconnected intelligence and electrification will be in the future of car manufacturing. Former Volkswagen chairman Herbert Diess has also pointed to intelligence as a decisive factor in the future of the automotive industry, citing Nokia as a cautionary tale for automakers (Automotive News Europe 2021)

© The Author(s), under exclusive license to Springer Nature Switzerland AG 2023
J. Y. Yang et al., *Chinese Electric Vehicle Trailblazers*, Business Guides on the Go,
https://doi.org/10.1007/978-3-031-25145-0_5

> **"I think long term, people will think of Tesla as much as an AI robotics company as we are a car company or an energy company."**
>
> *- Tesla CEO Elon Musk*

> **"The real game changer is software and autonomous driving."**
> *- Former Volkswagen Chairman Herbert Diess*

The Chinese government also declared autonomous driving and intelligent transportation to be key areas for development in their 14th 5-year plan (Huld 2021). By 2025, the government aims to have mastered the overall technology of autonomous driving and various other key technologies. In addition, it intends to establish better independent R&D and production support systems and an industrial cluster of intelligent networked vehicles, as well as to complete the transformation and upgrading of the Chinese automobile industry.

As technologies in areas such as mobile networks and semiconductors continue to advance daily, the possibilities for development are endless. This applies in particular to China, the country with the largest population and the second largest gross domestic product (GDP) in the world. As a population that has seen more change and growth than any other in the past few decades, Chinese people have developed an openness to new innovations. This factor, alongside the Chinese government's constant promotion of research and development, has made China one of the most innovative countries in the world (Dychtwald 2021).

This has led to Chinese people taking a different view of the new generation of cars compared to the rest of the world. Established automakers regard EVs as only differing from ICEs in their powertrain, with EVs representing a more efficient and sustainable solution. By contrast, challengers like Tesla, NIO, and XPeng see EVs as a completely new kind of product—an intelligent device. China's National Development and Reform Commission (NDRC) even specifically mentions in its Intelligent Vehicle Innovation and Development Strategy document the gradual shift of cars toward becoming intelligent mobile spaces and application terminals (NDRC 2020).

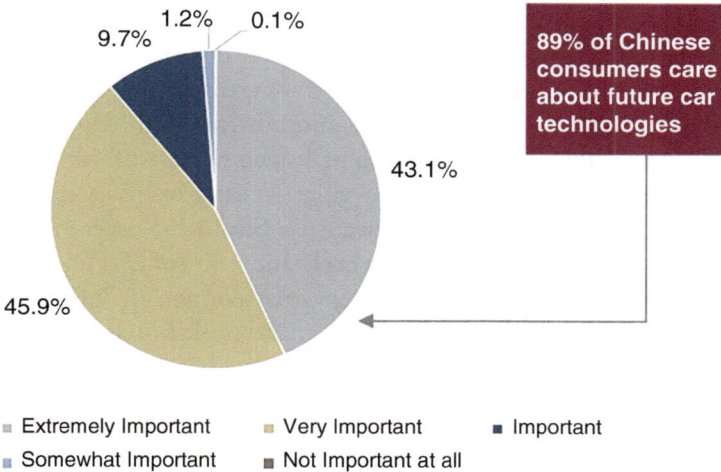

Fig. 5.1 Importance of advances in EV intelligence to Chinese consumers (D1ev 2021)

The advancement of EV intelligence is increasingly important to Chinese consumers, as shown in Fig. 5.1 (D1ev 2021). This has led to challengers gaining market share in the domestic market, while established players like Volkswagen rely too heavily on increasingly outdated purchasing criteria and consequently see their market share decrease. The Simon-Kucher and Partners Global Automotive Study 2022 echoes this sentiment, as China is among the countries that are most accepting of autonomous driving and human–machine interactions in the car (Gehring et al. 2022).

5.1 The Different Paths to Smartification

EV intelligence manifests itself in many ways, and Chinese automakers are exploring all the methods of integrating intelligence into their cars, secure in the knowledge that their compatriots are eager and willing to adopt these new innovations. The car, once purely a means of transportation, has now evolved to be so much more. The change the automotive industry faces is equivalent to what mobile phone manufacturers underwent as they transitioned to smartphones.

Nowadays, phones are required for much more than calls and texts, and watches are used for more than just telling the time. Likewise, modern vehicles need to be more than just a means of getting from A to B. This focus on using cutting-edge automotive technology to offer a unique product has played a huge part in the success of Chinese automakers, at least domestically. When criticized early in his career for lacking experience in the automotive industry, Shufu Li, now chairman of Geely, said that a car is "just four wheels and two sofas" (Young 2010). That design approach might have been good enough in the 1990s, but now, Chinese automakers are building smart, multifunctional terminals on wheels.

Chapter 3 outlined the different EV stakeholders, including automotive suppliers and mobility providers. As cars become smarter, avenues open for tech giants to enter the market. The new generation of cars they produce is much more complex, involving many different technologies including infotainment systems, self-driving and assisted-driving capabilities, and connectivity solutions. Huawei's business strategy for entering the automotive industry provides a great example of all the complex features that go into a modern Chinese car. The company has highlighted five main areas it intends to explore as part of its business strategy, as seen in Fig. 5.2 (Huawei 2020).

The acquisition of Meizu by Geely in June 2022 (Deng 2022) also showcases the changing nature of the industry. Meizu was once one of the most popular smartphone brands in China. Geely acquired Meizu to bolster the connection between its vehicles and intelligence systems, as well as to build a digital platform that can compete with that of its rivals. This is in line with the "Smart Geely 2025" strategy mentioned in Sect. 3.1. Geely is betting on a future in which operating systems in cars and smartphones are more integrated, and this acquisition is one way for them to bridge that gap. Meizu will remain as an independent brand, but the two companies will collaborate closely on areas like software (Liao 2022a).

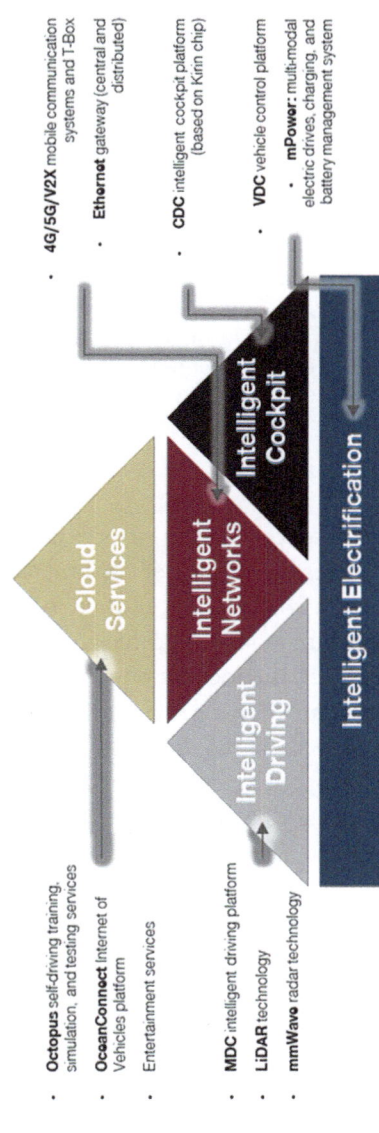

Fig. 5.2 Huawei intelligent vehicle business strategy (Huawei 2020)

Internet of Vehicles (IoV)

One factor that has been crucial to many developments in intelligent systems for EVs is the improvement of cloud computing and connectivity. The Chinese government is actively promoting the development of cellular vehicle-to-everything (C-V2X) systems, which would allow vehicles to communicate with the cloud, other vehicles, infrastructure, and pedestrians. In the NDRC's Roadmap for Intelligent Connected Vehicle Technology 2.0 (NDRC 2020), the government has set a target of 50% of new cars to be equipped with C-V2X terminals by 2025 (Dandan 2020).

It also aims for a new generation of wireless communication networks to be implemented, fostering the development of other technologies. China is well ahead of the rest of the world in this respect, with over 1.39 million 5G base stations as of late 2021, and approximately 450 million 5G terminal users (80% of the world's total) (Businesswire 2022). Many Chinese automakers such as NIO, SAIC, and BYD already market 5G capabilities as a selling point. However, the penetration rate as of 2021 was less than 0.4%.

Intelligence in EVs presents an array of opportunities involving many industries and technologies, as illustrated in Huawei's intelligent vehicle business strategy. The future of the automotive industry will rely on collaboration as it is brought together with other industries for potentially the first time. For now, however, the focus is on two factors—intelligent cockpit systems and autonomous driving. According to autonomous driving software start-up DeepRoute.ai (Cheng 2022), these are the two most important factors in intelligent vehicles from a customer perspective. The following two subchapters address these two factors in more detail.

5.2   Intelligent Cockpits

Chinese automakers are using advanced human–machine interface (HMI) systems and integrated apps to create intelligent cockpits that can provide a fully interconnected user experience. With the backing of Internet giants like Huawei, Chinese automakers have managed to turn cars from simple means of transportation into moving intelligent devices.

AIWAYS's newest EV, the U6ion, will be designed with an HMI dashboard with voice control and recognition. The dashboard will enable users to control both the car's driving and its entertainment functions. XPeng and NIO are also at the cutting edge of EV intelligence systems and are now developing a self-driving program on par with Tesla's "Autopilot." The dashboard developed by XPeng recognizes users and monitors everything from their music preferences to health. XPeng's proprietary operating system, Xmart OS, is already in operation in XPeng's G3 SUV, which has been well received in Norway.

Xmart OS

XPeng's Xmart OS In-car Intelligent System provides customers with a state-of-the-art HMI. Drivers can control the car using only the vehicle's voice assistant, which has a voice recognition accuracy of 98.6% (XPeng Motors 2022). They can even customize their voice assistant to suit their preferences, with each option employing human-like speech patterns and 14 emotional tones.

The central information display in all their cars is a vertical touchscreen that resembles an enlarged smartphone screen. On it, drivers can watch movies and TV shows, download apps, and play video games from the comfort of their seats. They can connect to social media and stay in touch with their friends and family or browse the web in the same way they would on their phone. Drivers can even pay using Xmart OS, which can be connected to AliPay. Furthermore, XPeng has joined Tesla as one of the few automakers to offer over-the-air (OTA) updates, so their customers will always have access to the latest version of the software.

XPeng is just one of the many Chinese automakers to focus on improving the intelligence of their cars, as the Chinese market is responding well to these features. XPeng founder Xiaopeng He sees intelligence as the true differentiating factor between automakers currently, as electrification is gradually being mastered across the world (XPeng Motors 2020). Intelligent systems are the logical next step. More and more features currently available on mobile phones will soon be in people's cars as well.

"The EV market in China will likely reach an upward inflection point in one to two years, in our view, and the real differentiation for players will be on smart and autonomous capabilities, not just electric cars."

- Xpeng Founder Xiaopeng He

5.3   Autonomous Driving

Today, autonomous driving is the topic of much discussion, as automakers around the world race to be the first to develop a fully autonomous vehicle. The Chinese government set out a series of goals in their Roadmap for Intelligent Connected Vehicle Technology 2.0 (Li 2020) mentioned previously. By 2025, it wants intelligent connected vehicles with partially automated driving and conditional automated driving capabilities to account for more than 50% of all vehicle sales. Furthermore, it wants to realize the commercial application of vehicles with highly automated driving capabilities, initially in specific scenarios and restricted areas, before expanding to a wider scope. China is the ideal place to launch and develop autonomous driving, as there are fewer governmental regulations regarding testing. For example, as of August 2022, the city of Shenzhen has allowed driverless cars (Level 3) to operate on public roads in certain areas (Liao 2022b).

Although the word "autonomous" has often been the subject of recent discussion, there is little agreement over its exact meaning. To better understand how far development of a self-driving car has come, it is crucial to recognize the various levels of automation. The most universally acknowledged measure for automation in the world is the SAE Levels of Driving Automation™, in which automation ranges from Level 0 (no driving automation) to Level 5 (full driving automation). However, as of March 2022, the Chinese government has adopted a different, albeit similar, measure for automation. As seen in Tables 5.1 (Liang et al. 2021) and 5.2 (SAE 2021), the Society of Automotive Engineers' (SAE) definition is a

Table 5.1 Official Chinese taxonomy of driving automation for vehicles (Liang et al. 2021)

Level 0	Emergency assistance	Systems do not continuously perform lateral or longitudinal vehicle movement control in dynamic driving tasks but have the capability to continuously perform partial target and event detection and responses
Level 1	Partial driver assistance	Systems continuously perform lateral or longitudinal vehicle movement control in dynamic driving tasks under their designed operating conditions and have the capability to detect and respond to partial targets and events appropriate to the lateral or longitudinal vehicle movement control being performed
Level 2	Combined driver assistance	Systems continuously perform lateral and longitudinal vehicle movement control in dynamic driving tasks under their designed operating conditions and have the capability to detect and respond to partial targets and events appropriate to the lateral and longitudinal vehicle movement control being performed
Level 3	Conditionally automated driving	Systems perform all dynamic driving tasks continuously under their designed operating conditions
Level 4	Highly automated driving	Systems perform all dynamic driving tasks continuously under their designed operating conditions and automatically implement minimal risk strategies
Level 5	Fully automated driving	Systems perform all dynamic driving tasks continuously under any drivable condition and automatically implement a minimal risk strategy

Table 5.2 SAE levels of driving automation (SAE 2021)

Level 0	No driving automation	These features are limited to providing warnings and momentary assistance
Level 1	Driver assistance	These features provide steering **OR** brake/acceleration support to the driver
Level 2	Partial driving automation	These features provide steering **AND** brake/acceleration support to the driver
Level 3	Conditional driving automation	These features can drive the vehicle under limited conditions and will not operate unless all required conditions are met
Level 4	High driving automation	
Level 5	Fully driving automation	These features can drive the vehicle under all conditions

bit ambiguous and leaves plenty of room for interpretation. By contrast, the Chinese version of classification is more detailed and clearer.

Chinese automakers are integrating autonomous driving features into their cars in a race to be the first to achieve true autonomous driving. Thanks to the more favorable government regulations in China regarding testing and operation on public roads, Chinese automakers have an edge over their international counterparts. Baidu unveiled the Apollo RT6 in July 2022, which has reportedly achieved L4 automation. It is yet another addition to their fleet of self-driving robotaxis operating under the name Apollo Go, mentioned in Sect. 3.3. Since its initial launch in 2020, Apollo Go has expanded to 10 cities in China and given over one million rides (Doll 2022). With such positive early signs, many automakers are working on making autonomous driving a reality, including traditional automakers like Geely and start-ups like NIO and XPeng.

Artificial Intelligence and Deep Learning

The key to unlocking true autonomous driving lies in AI and deep learning (DL). Modern cars are equipped with a plethora of onboard sensors, ranging from lidar (light detection and ranging) and radar to cameras. While these cars are being driven, data from these sensors is fed back to the manufacturer and used to train the AI. Tesla says it employs 1000 people just to label the images that come back from the cameras of Tesla cars, annotating cars, trucks, traffic signs, lane markings, and more (Knight 2021). The more data Tesla gathers, the more accurately its neural network can identify different variables when driving and make appropriate decisions.

In the future, most cars will have an AI computer on board to process information from the sensors in real time. AI will be essential for full automation, as the car needs to be able to make decisions on its own based on the information it receives. NVIDIA is a market leader in AI technology, with NIO, XPeng, and Li Auto all using NVIDIA infrastructure in their cars. NIO's Adam supercomputer, which will run their proprietary autonomous driving algorithms, is built on four NVIDIA processors and can achieve over 1000 trillion operations per second (TOPS).

Advanced Driver Assistance Systems: The Easier Alternative

The jump from Level 2 (L2) to Level 3 (L3) is a big one and represents the transition from advanced driver assistance systems (ADAS) to autonomous driving. At L3 and above, the driver is not required to take control unless an emergency or a malfunction occurs. At L5, the driver is not required to take control in any situation. Currently, there are some cars on the market that have demonstrated L3 capabilities, such as the Changan UNI-T, which debuted in China. It comes equipped with 5 mm-wave radar sensors, six cameras, and 12 ultrasonic radar sensors (Changan Auto 2022).

However, L3 vehicles are few and far between on the roads, and full adoption of this technology is still years away. Several factors contribute to this lag, such as the research and development costs involved, stringent regulations to guarantee drivers' safety, and a general reluctance among customers to give up control of their vehicles (which they are required to do when using functions of L3 or above). L3 automation requires substantially more computing power, and the more removed the driver is from control of the vehicle, the more complicated the processes involved become. This has also led some automakers to reconsider whether to pursue L3 automation, since the costs may be too great to offset any benefits for the foreseeable future.

Instead, their focus has turned to L2+ automation, the intermediate step between L2, which has already been successfully developed, and L3, which remains out of reach. While L2 automation provides steering and brake/acceleration support to the driver, L2+ automation incorporates detection of surroundings and AI to further enhance safety and convenience. One example of an L2+ automation feature is the use of map data in lane-keeping assist to keep the car in the middle of the lane even where there are no or faded lane markings or during poor weather conditions. Crucially, however, the driver always remains in control of the vehicle.

Adoption of both L2 and L2+ automation increased significantly in China in 2021, with production of vehicles with these installations increasing by 153% and 227%, respectively, and the installation rate having increased by 6 and 0.8 percentage points, respectively. At the end of 2021, L3 automation was at an installation rate of 0.3%, while Chinese automakers are aiming to mass-produce L4 vehicles by 2025 (Research and Markets 2022).

Autonomous Driving as a Service

With the development of ADAS technologies and all the new features they offer, many automakers have seized the opportunity to adjust their business models and monetize this innovation. One emerging model is Autonomous Driving as a Service (ADaaS). Tesla, one of the market leaders, switched to a subscription service for their ADAS technology Full Self-Driving (FSD) in July 2021. Initially, this technology was only available in exchange for a one-off fee of approximately EUR 12,000. Now, Tesla offers this technology to their customers for a monthly payment of about EUR 200.

This approach is shared by many Chinese automakers. NIO and XPeng have developed the NIO Autonomous Driving and XPilot ADAS technologies, respectively, and intend to sell them using the same subscription model. The pros and cons of the model will be explored further in Sect. 6.2. There is still much debate in the automotive industry about whether subscriptions are the way forward. Li Xiang, founder and CEO of Li Auto Inc., made a forceful statement on an investor call in 2021, claiming autonomous driving would be a necessity in cars in the future. However, it remains to be seen whether the subscription model is the best way forward for implementing autonomous driving in cars.

> **"Autonomous driving is a safety feature; it will not be optional and there will be no subscription service."**
>
> *- Li Auto Founder Li Xiang*

5.4   Optional or Standard

It cannot be denied that many Chinese automakers have traditionally relied on benchmarks for product design set by other popular car models. These manufacturers select certain competitors and try to mimic their products—a tactic which often backfires. Their choice of main competitors is often questionable and the products they produce as a result fail to meet the expectations of target customers.

However, in the past decade, the Chinese automotive industry has undergone a digital makeover. The age of first-time buyers in China with enough disposable income to buy a car is decreasing. As most new customers have grown up in the smartphone era, they expect a modern EV to have digital capabilities. This has now largely become standard for Chinese automakers in the EV era. In-car voice assistants support drivers with every element of their daily lives, from selecting infotainment and paying for online purchases to delivering WeChat messages and sharing recommendations for where to eat and drink. Drivers can even activate autonomous driving mode, prompting sensors and software to kick in and take over controlling, navigating, and driving the vehicle.

Despite the complex technology manufacturers incorporate into their cars, the equipment and trim options available to Chinese customers are unusually simple. In contrast to their Western counterparts, which capitalize on each customer's willingness to pay by offering sparsely equipped basic models and a large variety of additional customization options, Chinese EV start-ups tend to leave little room for customization.

This strategy suits Chinese EV start-ups well, as it is essential for them to quickly determine the product-market. This is further exemplified by their smaller portfolio of EVs. NIO, XPeng, and Li Auto all have fewer than 10 EV models to their name. They do not need to meet every potential customer need with their first few cars—they just need to show that there is sufficient demand. As with most start-ups, the Chinese EV manufacturers are burning through their capital and have yet to turn a profit. For now, it is a wise move for them to keep their range of products simple and keep engineering and production complexity at a manageable level.

However, as customer awareness and knowledge about EVs continue to grow, Chinese automakers need to consider reviewing their features to align their product offering with customer demands and communicating the benefits of each option clearly, as overequipping the vehicles would be detrimental to both the customers' value perception and the automakers' profits. XPeng has begun this process with its P5 model, in which the interior can be reconfigured as a movie theater spanning its full width or a full-length private sleeping compartment. Furthermore, it has a built-in refrigerator and air fresheners with fragrance control (Callum 2021).

Ultimately, Chinese automakers are faced with a similar dilemma to that posed by EV ranges; they may indeed be able to improve this feature, but they have to ask themselves whether or not they really should.

References

Automotive News Europe (2021) VW CEO says smart cars, not EVs, are 'game changer'.https://europe.autonews.com/munich-auto-show/vw-ceo-says-smart-cars-not-evs-are-game-changer. Accessed 23 Aug 2022

Businesswire (2022) China automotive and 5G industry integration development report 2022: application of 5G-V2X will promote the realization of high-level autonomous driving. https://www.businesswire.com/news/home/20220523005608/en/China-Automotive-and-5G-Industry-Integration-Development-Report-2022-Application-of-5G-V2X-Will-Promote-the-Realization-of-High-level-Autonomous-Driving%2D%2D-ResearchAndMarkets.com. Accessed 23 Aug 2022

Callum B (2021) XPeng reveals latest P5 model with reconfigurable interior Automotive Interiors World. https://www.automotiveinteriorsworld.com/news/displays/xpeng-reveals-latest-p5-model-with-reconfigurable-interior.html. Accessed 23 Aug 2022

Changan Auto (2022). http://changan.com.cn/. Accessed 23 Aug 2022

Cheng E (2022) Chinese automakers want to bring assisted driving to the masses. CNBC. https://www.cnbc.com/2022/06/13/chinese-automakers-want-to-bring-assisted-driving-to-the-masses.html. Accessed 23 Aug 2022

D1EV (2021) 从百度营销报告多维度分析新能源汽车行业:用户到底都想要什么? (Multi-dimensional analysis of the new energy vehicle industry from Baidu marketing report: what do users really want?). https://d1ev.com/kol/141987. Accessed 23 Aug 2022

Dandan Z (2020) Roadmap lays out path for connected vehicles. China Daily https://www.chinadaily.com.cn/a/202011/16/WS5fb1d9c1a31024ad0ba94473.html. Accessed 28 Oct 2022

Deng I (2022) Chinese smartphone brand Meizu sold to carmaker Geely as smart vehicles become latest frontier for Big Tech. South China Morning Posthttps://www.scmp.com/tech/big-tech/article/3181624/chinese-smartphone-brand-meizu-sold-carmaker-geely-smart-vehicles. Accessed 23 Aug 2022

Doll S (2022) Baidu unveils Apollo RT6 level 4 autonomous robotaxi with detachable steering wheel. Electrek. https://electrek.co/2022/07/21/baidu-apollo-rt6-robotaxi/. Accessed 23 Aug 2022

Dychtwald Z (2021) China's new innovation advantage. Harv Bus Rev. https:// hbr.org/2021/05/chinas-new-innovation-advantage. Accessed 23 Aug 2022

Gehring M et al (2022) Global automotive study 2022. Simon-Kucher & Partners. https://www.simon-kucher.com/sites/default/files/2022-02/ Brochure_Automotive-Study-2022.pdf. Accessed 23 Aug 2022

HUAWEI (2020) Intelligent automotive solution 2030. https://www-file.hua-wei.com/-/media/corp2020/pdf/giv/industry-reports/intelligent_automo-tive_solution_2030_en.pdf. Accessed 23 Aug 2022

Huld A (2021) China's autonomous driving industry—an introduction for for-eign investors. China Briefing from Dezan Shira & Associates https://www. china-briefing.com/news/investing-in-chinas-self-driving-car-market/. Accessed 23 Aug 2022

Knight W (2021) Why Tesla is designing chips to train its self-driving tech. WIRED. https://www.wired.com/story/why-tesla-designing-chips-train-self-driving-tech/. Accessed 23 Aug 2022

Lambert F (2021) Tesla is becoming more of an artificial intelligence and robotic company, says Elon Musk. https://electrek.co/2021/04/27/tesla-becoming-more-artificial-intelligence-robotic-company-elon-musk/. Accessed 23 Aug 2022

Li M (2020) 《智能网联汽车技术路线图2.0》日前发布——汽车智能网联是未来竞争焦点 (Intelligent networked vehicle technology roadmap 2.0″ was released recently—intelligent networked vehicle is the focus of future competition). Govcn. http://www.gov.cn/xinwen/2020-11/19/con-tent_5562464.htm. Accessed 23 Aug 2022

Liang et al (2021), Taxonomy of driving automation for vehicles. The State Administration for Market Supervision and the Standardization Administration of China. http://c.gb688.cn/bzgk/gb/showGb?type=online&hcno=4754CB 1B7AD798F288C52D916BFECA34. Accessed 23 Aug 2022

Liao R (2022a) Founders of auto giant Geely buys Meizu as smartphone demand weakens. Dent Tech. https://techcrunch.com/2022/07/04/geely-meizu-acquisition/. Accessed 23 Aug 2022

Liao R (2022b) Real driverless cars are now legal in Shenzhen, China's tech hub. TechCrunch. https://techcrunch.com/2022/07/25/real-driverless-cars-legal-in-chinas-shenzhen/. Accessed 23 Aug 2022

NDRC (2020) 智能汽车创新发展战略(Intelligent vehicle innovation devel-opment strategy). Chinese National Development and Reform Commission. https://www.ndrc.gov.cn/xxgk/zcfb/tz/202002/P0202002245730589 71435.pdf. Accessed 23 Aug 2022

Research and Markets (2022) Chinese independent OEMs' ADAS and autonomous driving report, 2022. https://www.researchandmarkets.com/reports/5631510/chinese-independent-oems-adas-and-autonomous.   Accessed 23 Aug 2022

SAE (2021) SAE levels of driving automation™ refined for clarity and international audience. SAE International. https://www.sae.org/blog/sae-j3016-update. Accessed 23 Aug 2022

XPeng Motors (2020) Smart car enthusiasm in China gathers momentum. https://en.xiaopeng.com/news/news_info/3421.html. Accessed 23 Aug 2022

XPeng Motors (2022) Xmart OS In-car Intelligent system. https://en.xiaopeng.com/g3/xmartos.html. Accessed 23 Aug 2022

Young D (2010) Geely's folksy Li known as China's Henry Ford. Reuters. https://www.reuters.com/article/us-geely-volvo-newsmaker/geelys-folksy-li-known-as-chinas-henry-ford-idINTRE66L2ER20100722. Accessed 23 Aug 2022

6

Chinese Route to Market

Keywords Transactional business model • Subscription model • Vehicle applications • Fan economy • Gamification • Guochao • Influencer marketing • Community marketing • Extended customer journey

Though it may seem like a cliché, it is undeniably true that many things in China work differently compared to the rest of the world. This includes how people receive information and news, interact with brands, and pay for products. Marketing and sales strategies that work in the Western world will not necessarily have the same success in China, and the reverse applies as well.

As with any country or region, there are significant cultural differences that companies need to be aware of if they are going to find success in the target market. In the automotive industry, this applies especially to EV start-ups like NIO, XPeng, and Li Auto that are fighting to gain market

J. Y. Yang et al., *Chinese Electric Vehicle Trailblazers*, Business Guides on the Go, https://doi.org/10.1007/978-3-031-25145-0_6

share from traditional automakers and joint ventures. This chapter will explore several marketing and sales strategies that work or have worked exceptionally well in China.

6.1   Embracing the Mobile Era: The Rise of Super Apps

The population of China has quickly embraced the mobile era and all the technological change that has come with it. In response, companies have employed appropriate marketing and sales strategies. As of February 2022, China had just over a billion Internet users (Statista 2022), far exceeding their closest competitor, India. By understanding trends and the market, Chinese automakers have mastered all the available ways of reaching their customers. Each producer has a strong online presence, especially on social media like WeChat, the most popular mobile app in China with almost a billion monthly active users. By actively engaging users through digital and mobile channels, Chinese automakers can build a relationship with their customers and successfully penetrate the market.

The mobile era has also given rise to what are known as "super apps." Super apps are particularly popular in China, though the concept has also been gaining steam in Southeast Asia with the emergence of Grab and Gojek. The definition of super apps is not set in stone, but the term generally refers to an app that has many functions and features that are distinct from the app's core functionality. WeChat is one famous example of this, since the developers have successfully built a comprehensive platform within their app.

Case Study: WeChat

Founded in 2011 as a messaging and photo-sharing app, WeChat has since evolved to be much more than that. With over 1.27 billion users in 2021 (Iqbal 2022), WeChat is the most popular social network in China. This is especially remarkable considering that the majority of its users live in China, as opposed to apps like TikTok (over 1.2 billion users), whose users are spread out all over the world.

The potential behind super apps is slowly being recognized. Elon Musk (Tesla CEO) and Jack Dorsey (Block CEO) have both expressed their intentions to create super apps of their own. This will not be easy, however, as the rest of the world has yet to embrace the mobile era in the way the Chinese have. There are several factors to consider, such as governmental regulations and consumer skepticism.

> **"There's no WeChat equivalent out of China. There's a real opportunity to create that."**
>
> *- Tesla CEO Elon Musk*

One of the main features of super apps that has yet to find its way into international markets is an easy-to-use mobile payment system. WeChat includes its own payment mechanism, which allows users to make seamless transactions. This in turn enables companies to set up webstores within the app so that every activity involved in a sale, from marketing to selection to payment, is made in the same place.

WeChat even has 3.5 million mini-programs, which are mini-apps listed in a mini-app store within the app. These mini-programs alone carried out over CNY 2.7 trillion-worth (about EUR 391 billion) of transactions in 2021. The availability of all these different features within one app means that there is no need for users to use any other app.

The mobile era has given companies access to a whole new generation of marketing and sales strategies, such as influencer marketing and community marketing, which are explored further in the following subchapters. Automakers are growing increasingly aware of the power of super apps and interconnected platforms, which has prompted them to abandon the traditional transactional business model and instead take advantage of the Chinese people's embrace of the mobile era. The best example of this is the NIO App, which can be used as a vehicle-purchasing and management tool, a customer service portal, a social network, and an e-commerce platform.

6.2 Is the Transactional Business Model Outdated?

For a long time, the automotive industry has used a transactional business model. Automakers would manufacture their vehicles and then sell them to dealers, who would in turn sell them to consumers. Most of their revenue would come from the one-off sales of their vehicles. However, as time has passed, and technology has improved, new business models have evolved as well. E-commerce giants like Amazon have shown the way in digitalizing business models, optimizing the customer journey, and maximizing customer loyalty.

Once a company has acquired a customer, its goal becomes to retain that customer for as long as possible. If it is successful, it gains access to a reliable source of revenue and customer base, which allows it to benefit from positive network effects. Chinese automakers are revamping their business models not just to improve the customer journey, but to take full control of it, creating a long-lasting mutually beneficial relationship for the company and its customers. More and more companies are realizing they are letting recurring revenues slip through their fingers, a problem they are tackling by implementing a subscription-based business model. Many European automakers offer subscriptions to their customers, as shown in Table 6.1.

Table 6.1 Subscription model offers of selected automakers in Germany

	Conventional OEMs						EV-specific OEMs		
	Volvo	Audi	Ford	Mercedes	VW	Jaguar/Land Rover	Tesla	Polestar	Lynk & Co.
Subscription available?	Yes	Yes	Yes	Yes	Yes	Yes	No	No	Yes
Name	Care by Volvo	Audi on demand	Ford Auto Abo	Mercedes EQ-Abo	Abo-a-car	Jaguar & Land Rover Subscribe			N/A
EV-specific?	Yes	No	No	Yes	No	No			Yes
Minimum term (months)	3	4	12	6	3	6			1
Price model	All-in	All-in	All-in	All-in	All-in	All-in			All-in
Services included	Insurance, maintenance, wear service, registration, tires, taxes, Wi-Fi hotspot	Insurance, service, registration, taxes, tires, pick-up and delivery	Insurance, maintenance, wear service, registration, tires, taxes	Insurance, maintenance, wear service, registration, tires, taxes	Insurance, maintenance, wear service, registration, tires, taxes	Insurance, maintenance, wear service, registration, tires, taxes			Insurance, maintenance, wear service, registration, taxes, remote updates

Subscription Models

Subscription models have also made their mark on the automotive industry and can be split into two subcategories: car subscriptions and feature subscriptions. Car subscriptions have yet to take off in China, with only a few automakers using this model. The Simon-Kucher & Partners Global Automotive Study 2022 (Gehring et al. 2022) shows that Chinese people have the highest awareness of subscription models, though they also have the lowest estimated monthly vehicle cost and the third-lowest willingness to pay among all the countries surveyed, which suggests they find car subscriptions to be poor value for money.

By contrast, car subscription models are becoming more popular in Europe, with a wide selection of automakers beginning to implement them. While Chinese automakers are reluctant to offer this to their domestic customers, two automakers owned by Geely heavily market their own subscription models in Europe. Volvo offers subscriptions with *Care by Volvo*, and Lynk and Co. offers subscriptions as standard. The global vehicle subscription market size was valued at approximately EUR 4.02 billion in 2020 and is expected to grow at a CAGR of 22.8% to approximately EUR 31.15 billion in 2030 (Precedence Research 2020).

Chinese automakers are in a more advantageous situation when it comes subscriptions to the individual features in the car. Two examples mentioned in previous chapters were NIO's BaaS and Tesla's FSD. However, it is tricky for automakers to decide which features to monetize, as some customers see certain features as necessities instead of simply being nice to have. One example of a failed feature subscription model appeared in 2019, when BMW offered Apple CarPlay accessibility as a subscription to their customers. The policy was eventually repealed due to customer backlash (Espósito 2019).

The advancement of technology will only further drive the adoption of subscription models, including in the EV industry. As with many of the other changes happening in the industry, customers may be initially hesitant to embrace the subscription model. However, doing so would grant them greater flexibility, since they can try out the vehicle and relevant features without having to make a significant immediate financial commitment.

Companies want their customers to return to buy more of their products and use their services more frequently. They measure their success at this using a metric known as customer stickiness. This is the key motivation for companies to abandon transactional models in favor of subscriptions. Marketing their products as a service is one way companies have found to put this new model into practice. At the same time, Chinese automakers are looking to expand their capabilities and find different ways to reach their potential and existing customers, becoming much more than just simple automakers in the process. For example, XPeng describes itself as a "technology company at heart" (XPeng Motors 2022). NIO offers its customers much more than just a vehicle; with NIO Life, NIO House, and the NIO App, the start-up supports its customers before the initial purchase and continues to do so long afterward.

WEY, one of the brands owned by GWM, is en route to the European market at the time of writing. In their marketing efforts, they are heavily promoting their own app (My Wey – The Way. A Way Forward.) on both the Apple App Store and the Google Play Store. According to GWM Europe Head of Sales and Service Gerald Krainer, WEY is planning not just to sell the car, but to establish an ecosystem around it (Wehner 2021). At the time of writing, the only way to reserve a WEY Coffee 01 (sometimes called the WEY Mocca) before its launch is through the app. This means that the customer is onboarded with the company before they have even purchased a car. If a customer reserves a car, they also receive extra benefits such as service and maintenance packages or WEY Points that can be used in the company eStore (also available on the app). Customers can also collect more loyalty points by actively using the app, and these points can be exchanged for products and even additional vehicle functions. The app also gives users access to aftersales services and vehicle management, meaning that WEY is present at every step of the customer journey, from before the purchase to long after.

A model like WEY's works well in China because Chinese consumers are used to using super apps and other online methods for almost all their needs. It might take some time for Europeans and Americans to embrace this new way of interacting with automakers and dealerships, or they might never do so. Though the jury is still out on that question, an increasing number of Western automakers now have apps to go alongside their vehicles. How long will it be until using an app to purchase and manage a car is a necessity instead of an option? While the transactional model is slowly becoming outdated, it will not disappear entirely any time soon either. It has been a staple of the automotive industry since its inception, and the likeliest scenario is that the transactional model will coexist with the subscription model and any other new models that arise. Nevertheless, car purchases no longer have to be one-off interactions—even if a customer insists on paying a single fee for a car, automakers are ready to offer much more than that. The car is no longer just a means of transportation, and before long, old-school customers will find themselves having trouble interacting with the ever harder-to-define automaker of the future.

6.3   Fan Economy

One significant aspect that distinguishes marketing and sales in China from the rest of the world is the power of the fan economy. Simply put, the fan economy refers to the income generated by the relationship between fans and the people they follow. A study conducted by AdMaster and Weibo about fan economy revealed a lot of information related to this phenomenon. For example, up to 73% of fans would spend money on products associated with their idols (AdMaster 2020), a group not just limited to celebrities.

One very good example of this is the scandal surrounding *Youth with You*, a Chinese survival reality television series in 2021. The show's sponsor MengNiu, a major Chinese dairy brand, became involved in the voting system by placing QR codes to vote for contestants inside the bottle caps of their milk products (Ji and Zhang 2021). Videos soon surfaced of fans dumping large amounts of milk directly into sewers after having bought the milk for the sole purpose of voting for their favorite contestants. After severe criticism of the show and its voting system, *Youth with You* was suspended.

Another example of the huge impact a fan economy can have is the collaboration between Kentucky Fried Chicken (KFC) China and Pokémon when they announced in 2022 that, to mark Children's Day on June 1, they would randomly distribute Psyduck toys in set meals. The collaboration became an instant hit, and the hashtag *#Psyduck* received nearly 135 million views on Weibo on the day of the toy's release (Koetse 2022). People either bought many of the sets themselves or paid people to buy the meals for them until they found the toy. While the set meal itself sold for between EUR 9 and 16, the toy was reselling for as much as EUR 200 online.

Hiring a celebrity or key opinion leader (KOL) to promote your product is a common marketing strategy. It increases your brand outreach and helps to build a connection between the product and the customer. Though the practice is increasingly proving obsolete, it has also led to the rise of "influencers" on different social media platforms in recent years, as companies have started to realize the impact some people can have on the general population's consumer behavior.

Influencer Marketing

More and more companies are turning to influencers and key opinion consumers (KOCs). They represent the new age of marketing and bring advantages that traditional celebrity marketing cannot. The main advantage they deliver is authenticity, as influencers are seen as having a genuine interest in their fields and the relevant products. According to Morning Consult (2022), authenticity is the most important trait for influencers to have if they want people to follow them.

Although their smaller following means the reach of each individual influencer is smaller than a celebrity's, influencers can foster greater engagement from their followers, and their content is more likely to be directly relevant to those fans. This leads to a closer, more trusting relationship, where their endorsement is as highly valued as a recommendation from a friend. Furthermore, their smaller following is reflected in lower (or no) costs for the company in question to work with them, as there is less demand for their opinions.

By getting the right people to promote their product, companies can reach customers in a way that leads to conversions. This outcome might not seem so certain when it comes to products like cars. Intuitively speaking, products of fast fashion and other commodities may benefit more from influencers and the fan economy because they are typically impulse purchases—one click is all it takes to have it delivered. By contrast, buying a car is a much more drawn-out, elaborate process that costs significantly more time and money. However, the collaboration between influencer Becky Li and automaker Mini proves that influencers can still have an effect on the sale of cars.

Case Study: Becky Li and Mini

Becky Li is a former journalist and blogger with more than 3 million followers on Weibo and 4.5 million followers on WeChat as of 2018. With a large following and a strong influence over the consumer behavior of her followers, she partnered with automaker Mini that year in what would prove to be a hugely successful collaboration.

Becky Li listed 100 limited edition Mini Cooper Countryman cars on her WeChat page. Each was painted in a rare turquoise hue called Caribbean Aqua and were priced at CNY 285,000 (about EUR 41,000). Despite the high price tag, all 100 cars sold out within five minutes of posting, which is a testament to her influence on her followers.

In an interview with South China Morning Post (Powell 2021), she shared her thoughts on why she was so successful at convincing her followers to change their behavior. She named trust as the main reason her followers end up buying the products she recommends. She only writes about topics that interest her, and always tests any products herself before she recommends them. Her fans regularly write that she is like a friend to them, as she interacts with them through her own posts and comments.

> "For digital influencers like me, I connect to my readers because, like them, I'm also an average person. I'm not a pop idol. My experiences will speak to them in a more direct way."
>
> *- Influencer Becky Li*

The collaboration between Becky Li and automaker Mini clearly shows the power that influencers wield, even when promoting such expensive products as cars. Trust is a key factor in this, and brands would do well to capitalize on the relationship between influencers and their followers.

Though she is not particularly knowledgeable about the automotive industry, Becky Li managed to influence her followers to buy new cars. Within the EV industry, there are more specialized influencers such as Chang Yan and Emma Meng, known as EV Emma to her 950,000 followers (Powell 2021). Using the Chinese social media platforms Weibo, Zhihu, and Bilibili, she focuses solely on the EV industry, providing advice about EVs and dissecting the latest news and technological developments.

Another way influencer marketing manifests itself is through e-commerce live streaming. Chinese e-commerce giant Alibaba introduced Taobao Live in 2016, a live-streaming feature intended to complement one of the biggest online shopping platforms in the world. Today, Taobao Live is a mainstay among Chinese marketing and sales strategies, and live-streaming features are available on all major social media platforms, such as WeChat, Douyin, and Xiaohongshu (also known as Little Red Book). NIO and Tesla are two of the automakers that have joined in with this trend. During a live stream in May 2020 with NIO founder and CEO William Li and NIO owner Li Rui, NIO managed to rake in 320 orders (worth about EUR 18 million) and scheduled a further 5288 test drives.

Live streaming has independently found use among companies aiming to sell products and influencers trying to grow their fanbase. It therefore seems to be a simple proposition for both parties to combine their efforts and mutually support each other to reach new audiences. Chang Yan and Emma Meng focus solely on EVs, and their followers follow them because they have a genuine interest in EVs. Influencers like them act as intermediaries between automakers and consumers, and their opinions and recommendations leave a stronger impression on their followers than any celebrity could.

Community Marketing

Community marketing, in which a brand encourages the formation and growth of a community of its customers, is another marketing and sales strategy that has proven effective. Even without direct intervention from the company, communities form organically as existing and potential customers seek other like-minded people to discuss their purchases, problems, and recommendations with. Communities like this can be found all over social media in the form of Facebook groups, Reddit subreddits, Telegram groups, and more.

Companies can engage enthusiastic customers through community marketing. While this strategy shares some similarities with influencer marketing in the sense that the interactions are based on trust and relationships, the main difference is that the interactions are typically between peers and mostly organic. Furthermore, community marketing typically targets existing customers. This means that the strategy's focus is on retaining customers by enhancing user experience and customer satisfaction.

Case Study: NIO Community

NIO has implemented many services aimed at bringing their customers together. These include the NIO App, NIO Life, and NIO House. These services provide their customers with everything from clothing and food to childcare. For example, NIO Houses contain a café, a library, meeting rooms, and more for members to access.

Furthermore, NIO Credit and NIO's referral program help not only attract customers but retain them. In addition to their vehicles and aftersales services, these rewards systems have helped NIO build brand loyalty unseen anywhere else. Existing customers can earn points by recommending to friends and family that they book a test drive or buy a vehicle and can then spend them on NIO Life products. The success of their community-building initiatives is reflected in their sales channels. An impressive 69% of NIO's sales as of May 2022 came through recommendations from NIO car owners (163.com 2022).

As mentioned at the beginning of the chapter, China, including the country's automakers, has quickly embraced the mobile era. NIO has developed the NIO App in recent years to be much more than just a vehicle management tool. One of the first options users see in the NIO App is "Discover." When users select this, they are shown content recommended to them based on NIO's algorithm. This includes business news posted by NIO and posts from other users such as advice on what car to buy and how to get the most out of it—the so-called user-generated content (UGC). Users can interact with each other by leaving comments and sending private messages. They can also see events hosted by NIO and register through the app to participate without needing to own a NIO vehicle.

NIO even has a separate system for tracking engagement and interaction within the community called the NIO value. By being active and upstanding members of the community, users can gain NIO value, which grants them voting rights to influence major community events and access to exclusive events such as NIO Day (App.Nio 2018). Overall, the NIO App has been a huge success. According to NIO chairman and cofounder Qin Lihong, the NIO App had over 400,000 daily active users as of July 2022. At that time, NIO had only sold 217,897 cars cumulatively (Kane 2022), meaning it had almost twice as many daily active users as car owners, which shows the reach that an app can have.

Communities will always exist, and it is up to companies to take advantage of this. NIO is one of the very first automakers to go to such great lengths in building a community of their drivers. Founder and CEO William Li even credited the loyal NIO community for its part in saving the company when it was struggling in 2019 (Bloomberg 2021). Building a community has always been at the core of NIO's marketing and sales strategy, and the more people who buy NIO cars and enter the community, the more NIO benefits, as the members post more content and the company can host more events.

Gamification

Gamification describes the strategy of incentivizing people to engage in contexts using game mechanics. It utilizes people's natural tendencies toward competition, achievement, collaboration, and charity (Bursztynsky 2021) to increase customer engagement and drive sales. Elements of gamification can be seen in marketing and sales strategies all over the world, such as frequent flyer programs and loyalty reward points. These give customers incentives to make more purchases from a company or use a product regularly.

However, gamification is taken to another level in China. It manifests itself in many ways, including live-stream giveaways and actual games within shopping apps. On November 11, 2020, in conjunction with China's famous Double 11 shopping festival, Taobao released a game in which users would collect Meow coins to look after virtual cats and level them up. Users could earn these Meow coins by logging in everyday (increasing engagement) and sharing the game with their friends and family (increasing reach). At certain levels, users could receive red envelopes containing up to 1100 yuan in vouchers.

NIO has also introduced gamification into their marketing and sales strategy, and this is clear to see in the NIO value system briefly discussed in Sect. 6.3. To increase (positive) engagement, NIO rewards their users by increasing their NIO value when they carry out actions that can be divided into four categories: community interaction, community

4 Pillars of NIO Value

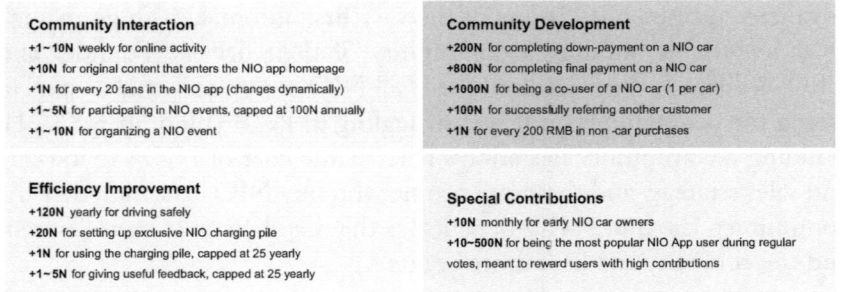

Community Interaction
+1~10N weekly for online activity
+10N for original content that enters the NIO app homepage
+1N for every 20 fans in the NIO app (changes dynamically)
+1~5N for participating in NIO events, capped at 100N annually
+1~10N for organizing a NIO event

Community Development
+200N for completing down-payment on a NIO car
+800N for completing final payment on a NIO car
+1000N for being a co-user of a NIO car (1 per car)
+100N for successfully referring another customer
+1N for every 200 RMB in non -car purchases

Efficiency Improvement
+120N yearly for driving safely
+20N for setting up exclusive NIO charging pile
+1N for using the charging pile, capped at 25 yearly
+1~5N for giving useful feedback, capped at 25 yearly

Special Contributions
+10N monthly for early NIO car owners
+10~500N for being the most popular NIO App user during regular votes, meant to reward users with high contributions

Fig. 6.1 NIO value scoring system (App.Nio 2018)

development, efficiency improvement, and special contributions. These actions range from simply logging in to referring friends and organizing events. The points system is explained in Fig. 6.1 (App.Nio 2018). The more points each user collects, the more likely they are to receive the final rewards. NIO App users compete with their peers to gain as high a NIO value as possible, all the while helping NIO improve by contributing to the community.

6.4   Guochao: National Trend

One of the more recent trends in China is "guochao." In English, it means "national trend," and it refers to a marketing and sales strategy where Chinese companies invoke patriotic sentiment when marketing their products, promoting Chinese culture through design details and marketing campaigns.

This is one of the ways Chinese automakers have managed to wrest market share from their Western counterparts in the domestic automotive market. Having started out as first movers in the EV industry, these automakers have built up their expertise and now produce cars of higher quality than ever before. While owning an imported car may have been a status symbol in the past, Chinese consumers nowadays are proud to buy

Chinese-made cars, and the manufacturers are acutely aware of what their Chinese customers want.

BYD is taking advantage of this trend with their "Dynasty" series of EVs. The name of the series itself is a reference to the dynasties of imperial China, reflecting a surge in patriotic feeling about that period in history. In a break from what Chinese automakers have done in the past, BYD uses Chinese characters in its cars instead of standard English words. The cars' design, which the company calls "Dragon Face," takes inspiration from traditional Chinese depictions of the mythical creature. The marketing campaign for BYD's cars also heavily featured the colors of the Chinese flag, red and gold, appealing directly to consumers' patriotism (Ofweek 2022).

BYD is just one of many companies tapping into people's love for their country, and guochao is a testament to the improving quality of Chinese-made products and the growing popularity they enjoy within China. Guochao represents something that global automakers must keep in mind when entering local markets. How are they going to appeal to the local customers? Can they leverage customers' patriotism for a successful marketing campaign? This is a strength of Chinese automakers domestically, but their foreign status may work against them if they decide to operate overseas.

References

163.com (2022) 蔚来凭啥有这么多死忠粉?看他们怎么做私域就知道了 (What makes NIO have so many fans? Just look at how they do private domain). https://www.163.com/dy/article/H70ILKVN0511805E.html. Accessed 23 Aug 2022

AdMaster (2020) 粉丝经济4.0时代白皮书 (Fan Economy 4.0 Era White Paper). 199IT.com. http://www.199it.com/archives/982550.html. Accessed 23 Aug 2022

App.Nio (2018). https://app.nio.com/content/1434229651?load_js_bridge=true&show_navigator=false&content_type=article&ADTAG=wechatfriend&share_uid=gC6Q6VJHrqU. Accessed 23 Aug 2022

Bloomberg (2021) China's answer to Elon Musk has survived once, but he has a fight ahead. Autoblog. https://www.autoblog.com/2021/06/13/william-li/?guccounter=1&guce_referrer=aHR0cHM6Ly93d3cuZ29vZ2xlLmNvbS88&guce_referrer_sig=AQAAAImqPToNK. Accessed 23 Aug 2022

Bursztynsky J (2021) Elon Musk praises Chinese automakers as Tesla works to improve company's reputation. CNBC. https://www.cnbc.com/2021/09/17/tesla-ceo-elon-musk-praises-chinese-automakers.html. Accessed 23 Aug 2022

Espósito F (2019) BMW will no longer require a subscription to use CarPlay in some cars. 9TO5Mac. https://9to5mac.com/2019/12/04/bmw-will-no-longer-require-a-subscription-to-use-carplay-in-some-cars/. Accessed 23 Aug 2022

Gehring M et al (2022) Global automotive study 2022. Simon-Kucher & Partners. https://www.simon-kucher.com/sites/default/files/2022-02/Brochure_Automotive-Study-2022.pdf. Accessed 23 Aug 2022

Iqbal M (2022) WeChat revenue and usage statistics. Business of Apps https://www.businessofapps.com/data/wechat-statistics/. Accessed 23 Aug 2022

Ji, Y & Zhang, H (2021), Hit variety show suspended after competition causes tons of bottled milk to be wasted. GlobalTimes. https://www.globaltimes.cn/page/202105/1222703.shtml. Accessed 23 Aug 2022

Kane, M (2022) NIO set new electric car sales record in June 2022. InsideEVs. https://insideevs.com/news/595703/nio-electric-car-sales-june-2022/. Accessed 23 Aug 2022

Koetse M (2022) KFC China's Psyduck Toy is a viral hit. What's on Weibo https://www.whatsonweibo.com/kfc-chinas-psyduck-toy-is-a-viral-hit/. Accessed 23 Aug 2022

Morning Consult (2022) The influencer report engaging Gen Z and Millennials. https://morningconsult.com/influencer-report-engaging-gen-z-and-millennials/. Accessed 23 Aug 2022

Ofweek (2022) 国潮风助推中国自主品牌汽车大发展 (National trend to promote the development of China's own brand car). Nevofweek.com https://nev.ofweek.com/2022-06/ART-71011-8420-30565659.html. Accessed 23 Aug 2022

Powell S (2021) Becky Li, Chinese KOL who sold 100 cars online in four minutes, on brands' new tool to gauge influence: 'They are cruel'. South China Morning Post https://www.scmp.com/lifestyle/fashion-beauty/article/3122361/becky-li-chinese-kol-who-sold-100-cars-online-four-minutes. Accessed 23 Aug 2022

Precedence Research (2020) Vehicle subscription market size, share, trends, growth 2021–2030. https://www.precedenceresearch.com/vehicle-subscription-market. Accessed 23 Aug 2022

Statista (2022) Countries with the largest digital populations in the world as of January 2022. https://www.statista.com/statistics/262966/number-ofrev-internet-users-in-selected-countries/. Accessed 23 Aug 2022

Wehner A (2021) Bei Wey soll die Community entscheiden, wie die Autos heißen (At Wey, the community should decide what the cars are called). https://www.next-mobility.de/bei-wey-soll-die-community-entscheiden-wie-die-autos-heissen-a-1053874/. Accessed 23 Aug 2022

XPeng Motors (2022) Future mobility explorer. https://heyxpeng.com/brand?prentId=5. Accessed 23 Aug 2022

7

Avoiding the Innovation Curse

Keywords Pricing • Price before product • Profit driver • Innovation curse • Pricing pitfalls • Extended customer journey • Pricing model flexibility

It is a sad reality that most innovations fail. According to Simon-Kucher and Partners, 72% of all new products flop, as most companies fail to successfully position their products on the market (Tacke et al. 2014). Many companies do a poor job of integrating customer value and pricing policies into their innovation process, meaning that their new products often do not fulfill profit targets.

> "Most companies deal with product pricing and marketing when it's already too late – often right before the launch."
>
> *- Simon-Kucher & Partners Managing Partner David Vidal*

Pricing is and always has been the biggest profit driver, and the results of the Simon-Kucher Global Pricing Study consistently highlight the

J. Y. Yang et al., *Chinese Electric Vehicle Trailblazers*, Business Guides on the Go, https://doi.org/10.1007/978-3-031-25145-0_7

price wars many companies experience. While the number of companies reporting increased price pressure has dropped over the years, the majority are still experiencing the effects.

When it comes to monetization strategy, the best approaches can be summarized as "build product to value" and "price before product." That is because when customers make purchasing decisions, they compare the product or service's price against its perceived value. Features therefore should not be included just because they are technically feasible, but because they provide a solution to a major issue for customers that they are willing to pay for. Through value-based pricing, companies can ensure they provide the right product at an appropriate price that does not "rip off" customers. Compared to their European counterparts, Chinese automakers are masters of this strategy.

7.1   Price Before Product

The foundation of a successful pricing strategy lies in a detailed understanding of the customers, and this is a lesson most Chinese automakers have taken to heart—adopting a customer-centric approach to their product design. They absorb input from customer research and tailor their offerings even in the early stages of product design. If their product offerings match customer demands, it is much easier to charge a price both the buyer and seller think is fair. Thus, the clearer an idea companies have of their target customers' ultimate willingness to pay, the easier they find it to design their products. The customer-centric approach taken by Chinese automakers is compared to the traditional approach in Fig. 7.1 (Yang and Gu 2021).

This chapter explores two cases of Chinese automakers that have followed these different paths to price their products in accordance with their targeted customer segments. However, to understand their pricing strategies, an overview of the customer segmentation in the Chinese EV market is essential.

As seen in Fig. 7.2 (Yang and Gu 2021), Chinese EV customers can be divided into four categories based on the type of vehicle they want to buy: plug-in-hybrid electric vehicles (PHEV), small pure EVs, midsize

Internal (product) focus:
We had a great idea and have developed this product – who will the customer be?

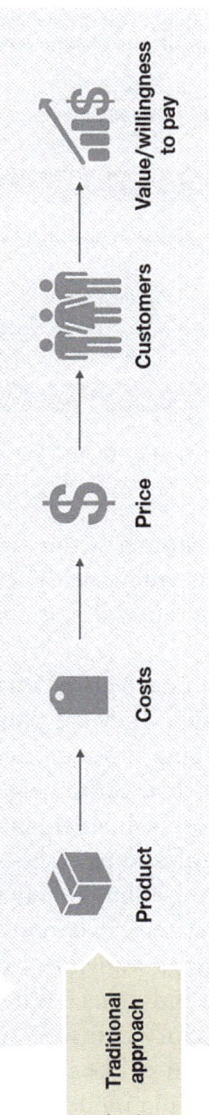

External (customer value) focus:
Which customers/customer groups benefit the most from potential products, and what is their willingness to pay?

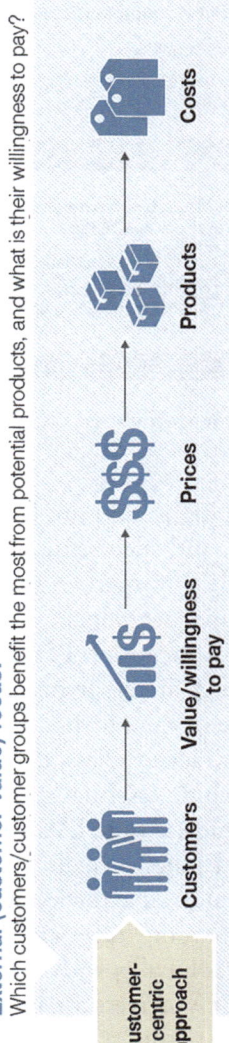

Fig. 7.1 Requirement for successful price models—make customer value the focus (Yang and Gu 2021)

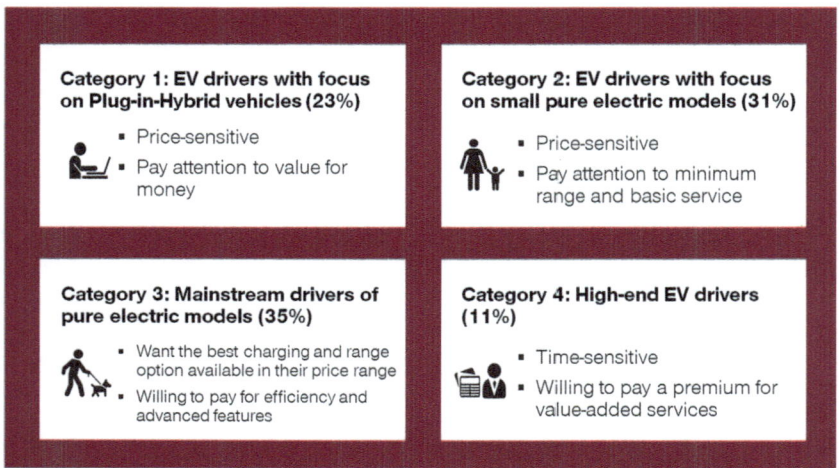

Fig. 7.2   Consumer segments of Chinese EV owners (Yang and Gu 2021)

pure EVs, and high-end pure EVs. Each customer segment has different characteristics, and successful automakers ensure that the entire process of bringing an EV to market, from design to aftersales, is adapted to one of these consumer segments.

The first two categories, PHEV drivers and drivers of small pure EVs, tend to be young drivers living in small cities. They are more concerned about the price of the car than battery charging times or high-end value-added services. Nevertheless, they still want their car to be good value for money and include essential services, such as 24-h emergency assistance.

Drivers of midsize pure EVs are young professionals living in big cities. They can afford a higher quality of life and are willing to pay for advanced features, but not at an extortionate cost. They tend to choose models with the shortest charging time and longest range available to them at an affordable price. Finally, with high incomes and a social status to uphold, high-end pure EV drivers are looking for luxury items. As such, they are willing to pay a premium for value-added features like connectivity. These preferences allow for a more complicated pricing model, as used by companies like NIO.

Case Study: Chinese EV Manufacturers: Premium Pricing or Budget Pricing?

Chinese EV makers can attribute much of their success to how well they adapt their pricing strategies to a particular consumer segment. They focus either on low-end segments or create new demand by producing high-end cars with advanced value-added features.

Premium Pricing: NIO

NIO is undoubtedly targeting high-end EV consumers, having priced its ES8 at around CNY 448,000 (about EUR 65,000). NIO is not a pure auto-maker by any traditional measure. Its origins are as a technology company, and it has inherited an innovative spirit from that background. The company hopes to replicate the success of Apple, which, with its revolutionary app store and unique offline customer experience, has introduced to its industry a new business model combining software, hardware, and services.

NIO offers unique and innovative features and services, making it an attractive luxury brand. Its internally developed driving assistance system, NIO Pilot, has 24 functions, including automatic parking and navigation. NIO's user system is also getting new features. As discussed in Chap. 6, NIO's growing community, well-developed app, points system, and subsidiaries fill the remaining gaps in NIO's offers. Using Apple as a benchmark, it is possible to see how NIO is succeeding in the market while charging premium rates for their products.

Budget Pricing: Wuling

Wuling sets itself apart from other Chinese automakers by offering products at extremely low prices. Although it is not well known outside of China, the Wuling Hongguang Mini is now China's most popular EV. In fact, Wuling made history in 2020 by beating Tesla's sales figures for the entire year in just six months (Ulrich 2021).

The ultra-low price of approximately EUR 4750 is the main reason for the Wuling Hongguang Mini's popularity, which has earned it recognition as the "people's car." Wuling has a clear target customer segment—the younger generation, especially first-time mothers. It has designed the Wuling Hongguang Mini accordingly to suit what its target customers use their cars for.

For example, the central information display has been removed from the Wuling Hongguang Mini, since most customers only use the car for short commutes in familiar surroundings. The central information display typically shows navigation and entertainment functions, so it is not a necessity for these customers. By the same logic, the seemingly poor range of less than 200 km is not a major drawback.

To allay customers' concerns about the quality of their cheap products, Wuling offers a power battery warranty of eight years or 120,000 km, in addition to fast door-to-door repair and free round-the-clock roadside assistance.

7.2   Pricing Pitfalls to Avoid

The two case studies in Sect. 7.1 are examples of Chinese automakers that stand out from the competition by identifying their target customer segment and tailoring their products to customers' price points and desired features. Wuling focuses on the low-end segment, which has no need for premium features and instead demands vehicles that can contend with urban mobility and short-range commuting. By contrast, NIO tries to create demand for high-end EVs with advanced connectivity features and other options to differentiate itself from its competitors.

However, the customer-centric approach is a double-edged sword. Many EV manufacturers fail because they do not fully understand who their target customers should be, resulting in an indistinctive end product. It is also common for manufacturers to define the price level purely based on benchmarking, resulting in a price that is in line with the product's competitive positioning but not its actual value. In taking this approach, Chinese manufacturers are faced with four common pitfalls, especially when they expand overseas:

Automakers Do Not Take Willingness to Pay into Account
As a new entrant from a developing market, one strategy might be to undercut competitors on price in the hope that international customers will change their brand preferences in return for a good deal. However, aggressive pricing can be detrimental to a brand's image. For example, in Germany, where price is considered a strong indicator of quality and status, an ultra-low pricing strategy might not pay off. Because EV producers are operating in a relatively new market, they need to be especially careful, as pricing their EVs against traditional competitors could underestimate customers' willingness to pay and leave significant earnings potential untapped.

Automakers Set Prices too High

Pricing can also go in the other direction and be too ambitious. Some Chinese automakers believe that outfitting their vehicles with every imaginable feature is essential if they want to demand a high price, and one-size-fits-all pricing models for their entire portfolio are commonplace. However, this is not reflected in what customers actually want. According to the Simon-Kucher Global Pricing Study, 68% of innovations in the automotive industry fail to reach their intended targets, indicating that automakers do not effectively communicate the advantages of features of their products or even build the wrong product entirely (Hudelmaier and Sarry 2019). Understanding the price–value relationship is a crucial input for product design.

Large Discounts Undermine the List Price

Companies that set overly ambitious pricing targets usually end up forcing dealerships into offering large discounts to boost sales. Customers can see a product's list and retail price and can therefore easily compare products using third-party online platforms. If a buyer discovers they could have haggled or searched for a better deal, they feel deceived about the vehicle's value. A large discount often has only limited effect in attracting customers. In fact, customers tend to distrust brands that cannot maintain their price integrity.

Strategy Misses Further Monetization Opportunities

Even in aftersales, pricing is not straightforward. Automakers are put under pressure from several angles. Firstly, putting a price tag on spare parts is highly complicated, and one model of vehicle can contain thousands of spare parts. Secondly, pricing methods often lack consistency and continuity, meaning that prices are decided on an ad-hoc basis. Finally, parts pricing strategies are often limited to cost-plus and competitive pricing and therefore fail to maximize profits. However, while there is room for improvement in aftersales pricing, automakers should also expand their aftersales business, e.g., with charging solutions and connected services.

7.3 Generating Income from the Whole Life cycle

The most successful companies do not just sell cars and then stop interacting with their customers; they provide support long after the purchase. In contrast to traditional automakers, which sell automotive parts and aftersales support to obtain profits, the new generation of EV producers focuses on both new vehicle sales and the inventory market, reflecting a strategy of changing revenue structures by providing value-added connectivity and aftersales services.

In Chap. 5, Chinese automakers' smartification of their EVs was discussed. The principal goal of smartification is to offer drivers a more intelligent, more comfortable, and safer driving experience, but these developments also heavily impact the business model of Chinese EV makers, especially with regard to their revenue streams.

Chinese automakers are gradually shifting their focus to other revenue opportunities during the product life cycle to achieve more sustainable margins. For example, after a purchase, they can offer on-demand services and features to consumers. Such features might include performance-boosting and battery-boosting software or ADAS. The three most successful EV start-ups in the Chinese market, NIO, XPeng, and Li Auto, all try to gain customers through EV sales and then offer value-added Internet services using the same profit model. Their revenue streams mainly consist of vehicle sales and leases, software services, and aftersales services, shown in Table 7.1 (Yang and Gu 2021).

This shift in revenue streams has begun to bear fruit. XPeng included software revenue in its financial report for the first time in the first quarter of 2021. In the same quarter, it released version 3.0 of XPilot, its internally developed ADAS, which the report showed had a cumulative payout rate of over 20% and even reached approximately 25% in March

Table 7.1 Revenue streams of the main Chinese EV start-ups (Yang and Gu 2021)

EV start-ups	EV sales	Other revenue streams
NIO	Sales of ES8, ES6, etc.	Primarily includes revenue from the sale of power packages and service packages, as well as some embedded products and services offered in conjunction with vehicle sales; embedded products and services include charging stations, vehicle-Internet connectivity services, and extended lifetime warranties
XPeng	Sales of G3, P7, etc.	Sales of the XPilot software; basic and plus versions of its Yuepeng service, which covers different usage scenarios for drivers, including vehicle maintenance, repair, charging, accident handling, and in-car entertainment; lifetime warranties of batteries; sales of charging stations and auto parts
Li Auto	Sales of Li One	Peripheral products and services, including embedded products and services from vehicle sales, such as charging stations, vehicle-Internet connectivity services, upgrades and extended lifetime warranties for owners, and stand-alone services such as Li Plus memberships

2021. This makes XPeng the first Chinese automaker to successfully boost its revenue with sales of software. XPeng's total software revenue was approximately EUR 30 million in the first quarter of 2021, allowing its gross margin to increase from 4.6% to 11.2% (China Economic Times 2021).

Xiaopeng He, the company's CEO, stated in a recent report that he believes Xpilot software will be an ongoing source of revenue for XPeng besides vehicle hardware sales (21st Century Business Herald 2021).

7.4 Providing Flexibility Through Pricing Models

How companies charge their customers is just as important as how much they charge them. Although one-time payments still dominate the automotive market, in recent years, there has been a shift from ownership-based to usage-based models, where possession of the vehicle is temporarily transferred to the customer, but the automaker remains the legal owner.

The most common type of transaction in the automotive industry is still a transferal of ownership, which has an advantage for manufacturers in that it boosts (short-term) cash flow. However, because they have limited control over vehicle supply (especially due to the used car market) and must contend with residual value backlashes, some automakers are finding more success with usage-based models. These not only give full control of the supply, but also allow automakers to capture the lifetime value of the vehicle.

Nevertheless, as mentioned in Sect. 6.2, Chinese automakers are generally not in favor of car subscriptions, because Chinese consumers show high awareness of subscription models while also showing limited willingness to pay. Meanwhile, the combination of both a one-time payment option and usage-based pricing (rental and subscriptions) is becoming increasingly popular among European automakers, as it leaves open the potential to transition to a usage-based model only fully under the manufacturers' control at a later stage. By following this approach, automakers can also attract new customer segments with a high willingness to pay, generating recurring revenues and increasing customer lifetime value.

As discussed previously, automakers should take note of the approach adopted by Volvo and Polestar, which are owned by Chinese manufacturer Geely and are currently leading the way in pushing sales away from ownership models and toward subscriptions and B2C/B2B leasing. To encourage adoption, Volvo shows customers a comparison of the costs associated with ownership and usage-based models, and has also run promotions where the first month's subscription is free of charge (Yang & Zuo). Polestar also markets its EVs in a similar manner.

> "Pure, progressive performance is our mantra. And it doesn't just apply to our cars. It applies to our entire approach. Fittingly, we offer finance options designed to remove the hassle from traditional car ownership, allowing you to focus on what matters: enjoying a Polestar."
>
> - Polestar Website

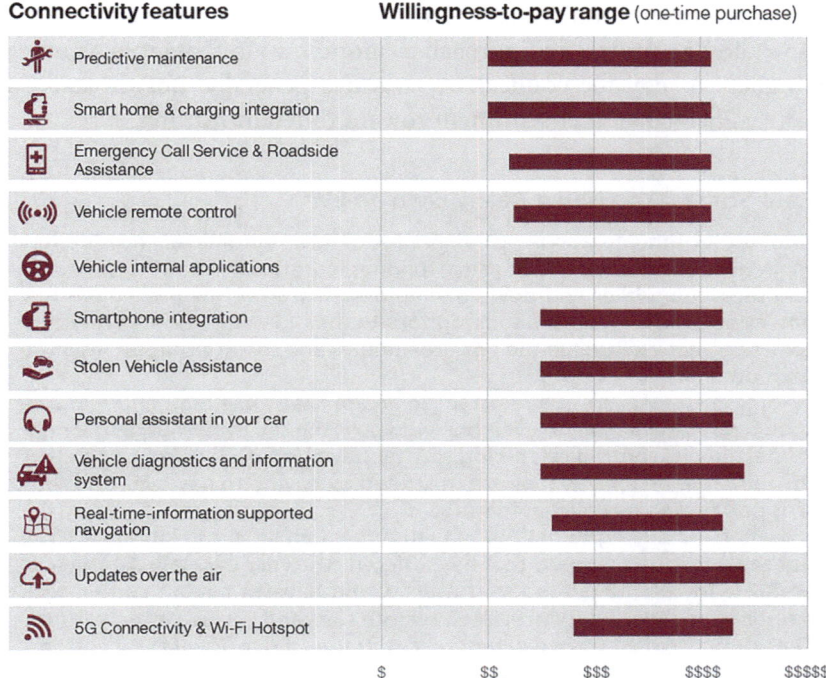

Fig. 7.3 Willingness to pay for different connectivity features (Yang and Zuo 2021)

Though Chinese automakers are apprehensive about vehicle subscription models, they seem willing to embrace the feature subscription model. NIO's BaaS is the best such example. Besides BaaS, many Chinese automakers are also starting to turn their attention to connectivity features. More and more are offering both one-time payment and subscription models for connectivity features to cover customers' preferences for payment options.

As mentioned in Chap. 5, it is critical for automakers to determine which features to monetize. One possible solution is to define item bundles. In a recent study shown in Fig. 7.3 (Yang and Zuo 2021), customers showed a similar willingness to pay for several connectivity features, indicating that they might perceive connectivity as a single feature and not be able to distinguish between individual elements. Therefore, instead of offering all features individually, bundling them into connectivity packages would be a promising approach to monetization that taps customers' willingness to pay for connectivity features generally, notwithstanding the diversified consumer sentiment toward different features.

Case Study: "You Never Really Own an EV"

As a result of the new subscription model, Chinese automakers now design their vehicles to work like big smartphones, constantly receiving software and security updates and downloading new features. However, there is a downside to taking feature subscriptions to their extreme, as not every customer segment will value the feature bundles and subscriptions as much as each other.

Some customers are still reluctant to accept that some high-end features should not be available to everyone who buys the car, even though the new model directly contradicts this logic. After having to pay a large sum to buy the EV in the first place, they are frustrated by having to pay recurring subscription fees to use certain features.

Section 6.2 highlighted BMW's failed Apple CarPlay subscription. BMW is not the only such company that has suffered customer backlash. At the end of 2021, Toyota announced that users would have to pay a monthly subscription fee for the newly released remote start and keyless entry features. The announcement caused widespread outrage among Toyota's EV customers, prompting the company to reverse course (Gunther 2021a).

There is a controversial debate going on about the new subscription pricing model. Customers who are not fully accustomed to the trend are still doubting its reliability and credibility (Gunther 2021b). Critics point to Apple as an example of what this model might lead to; iPhones only have a limited useful lifespan before Apple stops supporting them and providing updates—could EVs face the same fate in the future?

References

21st Century Business Herald (2021) 小鹏汽车软件卖了8000万!智能汽车盈利模式的想象空间有多大?(Soft revenue of 80 million! How much room is there for smart car profit models?). Finance.Sina. https://finance.sina.com.cn/chanjing/gsnews/2021-05-14/doc-ikmxzfmm2495388.shtml. Accessed 23 Aug 2022

China Economic Times (2021) 商业模式升级 软件收益计入营收或成小鹏汽车市值起飞起点 (Business model upgrade: software revenue may become the starting point of the take-off of XPeng's market value). Sohu.com https://www.sohu.com/a/468105595_115495. Accessed 23 Aug 2022

Gunther C (2021a) Toyota will make you pay monthly for your key Fob's best feature. Reviewgeek. https://www.reviewgeek.com/105381/toyota-will-make-you-pay-monthly-for-your-key-fobs-best-feature/. Accessed 23 Aug 2022

Gunther C (2021b) You do not really ever own an EV. Reviewgeek. https://www.reviewgeek.com/111381/you-dont-really-ever-own-an-ev/. Accessed 23 Aug 2022

Hudelmaier A, Sarry M (2019) Pricing an Innovation in the Automotive Industry—putting price before the innovation pays off. Simon-Kucher Insights. https://www.simon-kucher.com/en/blog/pricing-innovation-automotive-industry-putting-price-innovation-pays. Accessed 23 Aug 2022

Tacke G et al (2014) Global Pricing Study 2014. Simon-Kucher & Partners. https://www.simon-kucher.com/sites/default/files/simon-kucher_global_pricing_study_2014.pdf. Accessed 23 Aug 2022

Ulrich L (2021) China's most popular EV is no longer a Tesla. A new EV made by general motors and Chinese manufacturers underlines the virtues of Lilliputian size. IEEE Spectr. https://spectrum.ieee.org/chinas-most-popular-ev-no-longer-a-tesla. Accessed 23 Aug 2022

Yang J, Gu Y (2021) Pricing strategies: what the west can learn from Chinese car manufacturers. Simon-Kucher Insights. https://www.simon-kucher.com/en/blog/pricing-strategies-what-west-can-learn-chinese-car-manufacturers. Accessed 23 Aug 2022

Yang J, Zuo W (2021) Succeeding in Europe: how to build trust through price. Simon-Kucher Insights. https://www.simon-kucher.com/en/blog/succeeding-europe-how-build-trust-through-price. Accessed 23 Aug 2022

8

On the March to Globalia

Keywords Globalia • International expansion • Overseas expansion • Market entry • Market penetration • Brand name

Expanding globally has always been one of the biggest challenges that Chinese companies face. To date, there are very few Chinese companies that succeed in both domestic and international markets. For every successful expansion overseas, there are many others that fail. One reason for this lack of success can be attributed to governmental regulations, but another is these companies' inability to adapt their sales and marketing strategies to international markets.

A term coined by Hermann Simon meaning a globalized world.

J. Y. Yang et al., *Chinese Electric Vehicle Trailblazers*, Business Guides on the Go, https://doi.org/10.1007/978-3-031-25145-0_8

Case Study: Li Ning

One famous example of Chinese companies floundering when expanding abroad is the sportswear and sports equipment brand Li Ning. Founded in 1989 by Chinese Olympic gold medalist gymnast Li Ning, the company gained huge brand awareness when he lit the cauldron at the 2008 Summer Olympics in Beijing. Emboldened by the sudden fame and media attention, Li Ning set its sights on challenging established behemoths such as Adidas and Nike.

However, this endeavor ended in failure. Li Ning wound up making huge losses in the following years (culminating in a loss of CNY 1.98 billion in 2012) as inventory soared and it lost market share. Their expansion attempts in the USA ended in a complete withdrawal. The cause of this was Li Ning's botched internationalization strategy, in which they chose to enter the U.S. market through one of the most saturated sectors available—basketball apparel. Its products were sold exclusively online after a distribution deal with Foot Locker failed, which spelt disaster in an industry where looks, feel, and fit trump all other factors in a purchasing decision (CKGSB knowledge 2014).

Furthermore, Li Ning underwent an unsuccessful rebranding, which resulted in a logo similar to Nike's and a motto similar to Adidas's (*Anything is Possible* vs. *Impossible is Nothing*). What is more, the company abandoned its main (perceived) selling point of value for money, the very thing that had made it so successful in the first place. In its efforts to reestablish itself as a premium brand, Li Ning also raised its prices. It soon found itself stuck between a rock and a hard place—potential new customers still saw them as a low-end brand, while previous customers were unwilling to pay the increased prices (Waldmeir 2015).

The story of Li Ning should serve as a warning to other Chinese companies who are looking to expand, especially overseas. Misunderstanding the market and its own strengths proved to be the downfall of one of the world's most promising sportswear brands. However, rumors of its demise have been greatly exaggerated, and it has since recovered somewhat, at least within China. Li Ning has moved on since the events surrounding the 2008 Olympics and has developed new strategies that it has used to great success.

As Chinese automakers set their sights on international markets, they too will have to adapt their strategies. It will be essential for them to know their brand reputation and positioning and play to their strengths, all while understanding their target market and demographic.

8.1   Revisiting the Overview of EV Companies in China

Leading Chinese OEMs are already actively engaged in markets abroad. Conventional Chinese automakers have typically entered developing markets such as Russia, South Africa, Middle Eastern countries, and eastern European countries, usually with low-budget products. Now, Chinese EV manufacturers are hoping to win a share of the premium segments with advanced NEVs as well.

One success story is that of MG, which is owned by SAIC and has achieved remarkable sales in mature auto markets such as western Europe, Australia, and New Zealand. However, MG, like other Chinese EV producers, is faced with another obstacle that makes it comparatively difficult to enter the U.S. market (Stewart 2022). This is because in 2018, former president Donald Trump's administration imposed a 25% tariff on cars imported from China. Many electric car parts are subject to the same tariffs.

Because of this, many Chinese EV producers have made their first steps abroad in western Europe. The prospect of breaking into this competitive but bustling market is simply too attractive for up-and-coming manufacturers not to at least try to make inroads. As of 2021, many Chinese automakers have already begun doing just that. The first target was Norway, the most electrified country in the world, with EV sales making up 65% of all car sales in 2021. Norway incentivizes the use of EVs by taxing them at a low rate or exempting them altogether, and the Norwegian population is embracing electrification, making it the ideal beachhead for Chinese expansion.

Despite the optimism surrounding the potential within the European EV market, as of January 2022, it was still dominated by the usual automotive powerhouses, with BMW, Mercedes-Benz, Kia, Peugeot, and Audi leading the way. To date, more than 10 Chinese OEMs have launched, or are about to launch, EVs in Europe. Among them are some of the most well-known manufacturers, both new players and established ones, including NIO, XPeng, BYD, and GWM. However, using EVs to open the door to western Europe, particularly in the premium segment, is not an automatic recipe for success for all Chinese OEMs. Only Polestar and MG have managed to get their products into the top 20 best-selling NEVs in Europe. By contrast, other Chinese automakers have barely made an impression in Europe (Burgard et al. 2022).

There is no doubt that Chinese EV manufacturers are pioneers in the industry, advancing in areas such as range, connectivity features, and ADAS development. Both the marketing concept and portfolio of Chinese EV players should pose a tough challenge for traditional European OEMs. However, several obstacles remain. Without their natural home advantage, Chinese players will have to go the extra mile to succeed. The first difficulty they face is establishing a business structure, starting from the basics such as sales, aftersales, and call centers.

The traditional three-tier sales model, in which automakers sell their vehicles to dealers and dealers sell on to customers, seems to be losing popularity as the new crop of electric-vehicle-only manufacturers choose to sell directly to the public. As touched on in previous chapters, Chinese automakers have also chosen to take on the job of selling their vehicles themselves, so that they have direct control over their brand image and price integrity and can maintain a direct relationship with their customers.

Nevertheless, dealerships still seem to have some role to play in international markets. According to plans for expanding EV sales into European markets set out by GWM, one of the largest automakers in China, its next step will be to form a strategic partnership with Emil Frey, Europe's largest car dealer group. Emil Frey will be responsible for the distribution of GWM's ORA and WEY brands.

GWM has already expanded well beyond the Chinese market, but few EVs have made their mark in international markets so far, especially in Europe. Having already experienced the challenge of establishing its own sales and service capacities in a new market, GWM decided to recruit a dealer to help alleviate the difficulties (Doll 2022). Fellow Chinese EV producer XPeng also announced similar collaboration agreements with Emil Frey Nederland NV to distribute its vehicles in the Netherlands and with the dealer group Bilia in Sweden (Eddy 2022).

In a time when more and more manufacturers are turning to direct sales, is this cooperation with dealers a compromise? For now, it is impossible to tell, as there are also new business models emerging from the traditional dealership sales model, such as the agency model. While some new entrants are selling directly to consumers online with no third-party involvement, many established automakers have chosen to maintain their trusted dealer networks. Lotus, for example, contracts with dealerships to offer test drives and help with the sales process, while Lotus itself retains ownership of the vehicles and signs sales contracts directly with its customers. In this case, dealers only receive a service fee, instead of making a direct profit from the sale—the so-called agency model, which Volkswagen has also recently been using in experiments with its ID Family.

For established automakers that have relied on the traditional dealership model for decades, the market entry of EVs is the ideal catalyst for transitioning to the agency model, since it allows them to start small. From the customers' perspective, buying an EV for the first time is more complicated than buying an ICE vehicle because they need help to arrange home-charging solutions and advice on how to drive to maximize their range. The agency model could therefore provide them with the support they need. It remains to be seen if the agency model could pave the way forward for Chinese automakers in Europe.

8.2 An Overview of Chinese EV Players' Footprint in Europe

OEMs Geely and SAIC were among the first Chinese players in the automotive industry to put down roots in Europe. Their presence in the region dates back to 2017, almost 2 years before other Chinese companies followed. Through mergers and acquisitions, Geely now owns the European brands Volvo, Polestar, and Lotus. Volvo and Polestar have been particularly successful within Europe (Sebastian 2021). Similarly, SAIC operates in Europe through two European brands: MG and Maxus. SAIC plans to launch more models and establish more marketing and service outlets within Europe to accelerate its development (SAIC 2021). These moves are shown in Table 8.1.

Compared to Geely and SAIC, other Chinese automakers are relative newcomers to this market, which is still dominated by foreign car brands.

Table 8.1 Moves in Europe by automakers Geely and SAIC

Time	Chinese EV company	Move in Europe
June 2017	Geely	Polestar was established as a new, stand-alone Swedish premium electric vehicle brand (Geely 2022)
October 2017	Geely	Polestar unveils its first electric vehicle, the Polestar 1 (Polestar 2017)
October 2018	SAIC	Maxus Motors launches its first electric vehicle, the SAIC Maxus EV80 (SAIC MAXUS 2018)
May 2019	SAIC	MG Motor debuts its first all-electric SUV, the MG ZS EV (Kane 2019)
October 2019	Geely	Volvo unveils its first electric vehicle, the XC40 Recharge (Volvo Cars 2019)
June 2022	Geely	Polestar goes public on NASDAQ stock exchange after merging with a special purpose acquisition company (SPAC) (Polestar 2022)
July 2022	Geely	Volvo announces plans to build a new factory for all-electric vehicles in Slovakia, with construction beginning in 2023 and production in 2026 (Hampel 2022a)

Their foundations in Europe were laid in 2021, and most of them have already announced further plans to strengthen their presence. Their moves in Europe are shown in Table 8.2.

8.3   What Has Worked and What Has not

There is still a long way to go for Chinese automakers within the European market, especially for EV start-ups. With expansion efforts ramping up in recent years, the sales figures in 2021 show a general upward trend, even if the growth is inconsistent from month to month. It remains to be seen if the Chinese EV start-ups' forays into European markets will ultimately be a success.

One key factor in automakers' success is their brand name. The sales of Volvo, Polestar, and MG vehicles, even though they are owned by Chinese automakers, far exceed those of purely Chinese brands. In the past, Chinese cars have had a poor reputation, whereas European juggernauts like BMW and Daimler were seen as the go-to brands by most Europeans.

Table 8.2   Moves in Europe by up-and-coming automakers

Time	Chinese EV company	Move in Europe
August 2021	BYD	BYD Tang SUV is launched in Norway (BYD 2021)
September 2021	GWM	GWM establishes their office in Munich and presents a Wey-branded plug-in hybrid SUV and an Ora-branded full-electric model at the IAA automotive trade show in Munich
September 2021	NIO	NIO ES8 is launched in Norway (NIO 2021)
November 2021	NIO	NIO launches a partnership with Shell to collaborate on charging and battery-swapping facilities (Hampel 2021)
October 2021	XPeng	XPeng launches its electric P7 sedan in Norway (XPeng 2021)
January 2022	NIO	NIO launches its first battery-swapping station in Norway (Kane 2022)
February 2022	Dongfeng	Dongfeng announces plans to enter the European market beginning in Norway with their subsidiary Voyah (Randall 2022)
February 2022	XPeng	XPeng signs agreements with European retail companies Billa and Emil Frey to sell their cars in Sweden and the Netherlands, respectively. It plans to open retail stores in The Hague and Stockholm (Roberts 2022)
March 2022	BYD	BYD announces a partnership with Shell to build an EV charging network in Europe and develop fleet and charging solutions (BYD 2022a)
March 2022	NIO	NIO announces plans to enter four new European markets—Germany, the Netherlands, Sweden, and Denmark. Sales in Germany are expected to start in Q4 2022 (Hampel 2022b)
April 2022	GWM	GWM enters into a strategic partnership with Europe's largest car dealer group, Emil Frey, to distribute their Ora and Wey brands
April 2022	GWM	GWM plans to open brand experience centers in Munich and Berlin as part of its plan to build a "lifestyle ecosystem" for European customers
May 2022	XPeng	XPeng opens its first European experience store in Oslo, Norway (XPeng 2022)
June 2022	Dongfeng	Dongfeng's subsidiary Voyah opens a showroom in Norway and unveils the electric "Free" SUV (APO 2022)
July 2022	BYD	BYD selects Louwman, one of Europe's largest automotive companies, as its national dealership partner in the Netherlands. Louwman will manage sales online and offline as well as aftersales services to customers in the Netherlands, with the first BYD store opening in Amsterdam (BYD 2022b)

The gulf in perception between these brands was not helped by incidents such as the failed crash tests conducted by Chinese automakers Jiangling Motors and Brilliance in Europe in 2006 and 2007, respectively. Europeans' loyalty to local brands has thwarted all attempts by Chinese automakers to enter the European market and forced many to pull out before ever making a mark.

However, things are different now. Chinese automakers have been minor players when it comes to the market for ICE vehicles, but they are now at the forefront of the contemporary electrification trend. The image of Chinese manufacturers is slowly changing across the world—once seen as archetypal copycats and purveyors of poor-quality goods, Chinese automakers have since rapidly developed and are now getting recognition not just from consumers, but other automakers too. More and more companies are willing to partner with Chinese automakers, which in turn enhances their reputation and provides them with market access they would not otherwise have.

There are several lessons to be learned from the strategies that Chinese automakers have used without success to break into the European market. Nevertheless, the automotive industry is also changing—for example, with the decline of dealers and the rise of marketing opportunities offered by digitalization, such as fan economy and lifestyle focus. It is too soon to say if Chinese EVs will take over Europe—but the chances of that happening are much better than ever before.

References

APO (2022) VOYAH FREE opened in Europe, and VOYAH showroom kicked off. Afr Bus. https://african.business/2022/06/apo-newsfeed/voyah-free-opened-in-europe-and-voyah-showroom-kicked-off/. Accessed 23 Aug 2022

Burgard J et al (2022) Quo Vadis, Chinese OEMs in Europe? Berylls. https://www.berylls.com/quo-vadis-chinese-oems-in-europe/. Accessed 23 Aug 2022

BYD (2021) BYD launches Tang SUV in Norway. BYD Newsroom. https://en.byd.com/news/byd-launches-tang-suv-in-norway/. Accessed 23 Aug 2022

BYD (2022a) BYD and Shell partner on EV charging across China and Europe. BYD Newsroom. https://bydeurope.com/article/416. Accessed 23 Aug 2022

BYD (2022b) BYD announces cooperation with Louwman for new energy passenger vehicles in the Netherlands. BYD Newsroom https://bydeurope.com/article/425. Accessed 23 Aug 2022

CKGSB Knowledge (2014) Chinese sportswear brand Li-Ning's long road to redemption. Forbes Asia. https://www.forbes.com/sites/ckgsb/2014/04/14/chinese-sportswear-brand-li-nings-long-road-to-redemption/?sh=222d1e4c1263. Accessed 23 Aug 2022

Doll S (2022) Chinese automaker Great Wall taps Emil Frey to distribute its EVs in Europe, beginning with Germany. Electrek. https://electrek.co/2022/08/09/great-wall-emil-frey-ev-europe/. Accessed 23 Aug 2022

Eddy A (2022) Great Wall partners with Emil Frey to distribute Wey, Ora brands. Automotive News Europe https://europe.autonews.com/automakers/great-wall-partners-emil-frey-distribute-wey-ora-brands. Accessed 23 Aug 2022

Geely (2022) Our brands/polestar. Geely Media Center. http://zgh.com/our-brands/polestar/?lang=en. Accessed 23 Aug 2022

Hampel C (2021) Nio & Shell join forces. Electrive. https://www.electrive.com/2021/11/25/nio-shell-join-forces/. Accessed 23 Aug 2022

Hampel C (2022a) Volvo will build electric cars at a new plant in Slovakia. Electrive. https://www.electrive.com/2022/07/02/volvo-to-construct-new-plant-in-slovakia/. Accessed 23 Aug 2022

Hampel, C (2022b) Nio expands into Europe and beyond. Electrive. https://www.electrive.com/2022/03/01/nio-expands-into-europe-and-beyond/. Accessed 23 Aug 2022

Kane M (2019) MG ZS EV to debut in Europe next week at London motor show. InsideEVs. https://insideevs.com/news/348899/mg-zs-ev-debut-europe-london/. Accessed 23 Aug 2022

Kane M (2022) Norway: NIO launches the first battery Swap Station in Europe. InsideEVs. https://insideevs.com/news/561903/norway-nio-first-battery-swap/#:~:text=NIO%20has%20officially%20launched%20the,few%20kilometers%20north%20of%20Drammen. Accessed 23 Aug 2022

NIO (2021) NIO ES8 launches in Norway. NIO Newsroom. https://www.nio.com/news/nio-es8-launches-nio-house-oslo. Accessed 23 Aug 2022

Polestar (2017) Polestar unveils its first car—the polestar 1—and reveals its vision to be the new electric performance brand. CISION PR Newswire. https://www.prnewswire.com/news-releases/polestar-unveils-its-first-car%2D%2D-the-polestar-1%2D%2D-and-reveals-its-vision-to-be-the-new-electric-performance-brand-651232153.html. Accessed 23 Aug 2022

Polestar (2022) Polestar lists successfully on Nasdaq. Polestar Press. https://media.polestar.com/global/en/media/pressreleases/654301. Accessed 23 Aug 2022

Randall C (2022) Dongfeng subsidiary 'Voyah' prepares for European launch. Electrive.https://www.electrive.com/2022/02/18/dongfeng-subsidiary-voyah-prepares-for-european-launch/. Accessed 23 Aug 2022

Roberts G (2022) XPeng expands EV sales in Europe. Just Auto. https://www.just-auto.com/dashboard/deals-dashboards/xpeng-expands-ev-sales-in-europe/. Accessed 23 Aug 2022

SAIC (2021) SAIC motor sets year-high monthly sales volume in Sep. SAIC Motor. https://www.saicmotor.com/english/latest_news/saic_motor/56113.shtml. Accessed 23 Aug 2022

SAIC MAXUS (2018) SAIC MAXUS brings EV80 to IAA 2018 in Hannover Germany. https://en.saicmaxus.com/news/201809/92.shtml. Accessed 23 Aug 2022

Sebastian G (2021) In the driver's seat: China's electric vehicle makers target Europe. Merics. https://merics.org/en/report/drivers-seat-chinas-electric-vehicle-makers-target-europe. Accessed 23 Aug 2022

Stewart M (2022) Chinese EV makers aim to sell cars in America. Capital.com https://capital.com/chinese-ev-makers-aim-to-sell-cars-in-america. Accessed 23 Aug 2022

Volvo Cars (2019), Volvo Cars launches fully electric Volvo XC40 recharge as part of new electrified car line. Volvo Cars Global Newsroom. https://www.media.volvocars.com/global/en-gb/media/pressreleases/259210/volvo-cars-launches-fully-electric-volvo-xc40-recharge-as-part-of-new-electrified-car-line#:~:text=The%20XC40%20Recharge%20is%20everything,on%20a%20fast%2Dcharger%20system. Accessed 23 Aug 2022

Waldmeir P (2015) Li Ning's rise and fall marks a cautionary tale. Financial Times. https://www.ft.com/content/0ece54f6-a03d-11e4-aa89-00144feab7de. Accessed 23 Aug 2022

XPeng (2021) XPeng flagship P7 smart electric sedan debuts in Norway. CISION PR Newswire. https://www.prnewswire.com/news-releases/xpeng-flagship-p7-smart-electric-sedan-debuts-in-norway-301410114.html. Accessed 23 Aug 2022

XPeng (2022) XPeng Oslo experience store now open with XPeng G3i and XPeng P5 available for local test drives. GlobeNewswire. https://www.globenewswire.com/news-release/2022/05/19/2446634/0/en/XPENG-Oslo-Experience-Store-Now-Open-With-XPENG-G3i-and-XPENG-P5-Available-for-Local-Test-Drives.html. Accessed 23 Aug 2022

9

Roadblocks to Success

Keywords Electric vehicle value depreciation • Increasing raw material costs • Electric vehicle governmental regulations • Data security • Cybersecurity

9.1 Value Depreciation

One challenge that the Chinese EV market is currently facing is depreciation, which greatly slows down the adoption of EVs. According to a survey by GeekNEV, a media group focusing on NEVs, ICE vehicles retain their value for longer than EVs. Among vehicles that are sold for CNY 100,000 or less in China, electric vehicles retain on average 67.8% of their value after just 1 year while ICE vehicles retain 74.3% after 3 years, as shown in Table 9.1 (Zhou 2021).

Traditionally, the reason for this depreciation has been that the rate at which batteries in EVs degrade is unpredictable. Furthermore, China's early subsidy regime led automakers to price models higher than they were probably worth. Now, as the end of all government subsidies approaches, Chinese automakers are losing more than just revenue;

Table 9.1 Difference in value retention between EVs and ICE vehicles (Zhou 2021)

Price level	Electric vehicle average value retention after 1 year	ICE vehicle average value retention after 3 years
Below CNY 100,000	67.83%	74.31%
CNY 100,000–200,000	59.72%	76.13%
CNY 200,000–300,000	68.20%	82.21%
Above CNY 300,000	68.30%	81.40%

without that support, they are being forced onto a level playing field with traditional ICE automakers, where customer awareness of depreciation has the potential to undermine the popularity of EVs and undercut the prices companies charge for them.

The government subsidies that fueled the industry early on have had a direct effect on how quickly EVs lose their value. In 2010, the Chinese government started offering subsidies to manufacturers of NEVs to promote their adoption both in public transportation and the private passenger car market, using funds from both the central and local governments. A turning point came in June 2019 when the government cut subsidies significantly. Before the reduction, some companies had scrambled to begin production of EVs so they could secure subsidies. Many of those cars ended up in smaller cities and rural areas, where they were sold at prices far below retail. The steep drops in prices in the secondhand market exacerbated the depreciation of EVs in China.

Buyback programs like XPeng's were created at least in part to offset the disincentive to buy a new EV caused by depreciation. In July 2019, XPeng owners who had bought the previous version of the G3 were outraged because the company began accepting preorders for an updated model just 3 months after their vehicles were delivered. They worried that the new version's launch would cause their cars to depreciate in value faster. Despite an initial attempt to appease their customers with a discount of CNY 10,000 (about EUR 1400) on the next XPeng vehicle they purchased, G3 owners were still angry, and XPeng ended up offering to buy back their vehicles. Buyback programs are money-losers for automakers because the actual value of the used cars is lower than their proposed buyback price.

To help EVs retain their value, it has been suggested that used cars be sold separately from batteries. NIO's BaaS model, where the car is sold with or without the battery depending on the customer's preference, has already made this possible. The car retails for between CNY 70,000 and 128,000 (about EUR 10,000–18,500) less than normal without the battery depending on its size. This makes NIO cars more affordable and eligible for Chinese government subsidies (NIO 2022). Decoupling batteries from vehicles also means that NIO can secure demand for battery upgrades, since the battery-swapping service will allow those who have signed up to upgrade their battery when a better one becomes available. Owners can also purchase new batteries individually, which helps preserve most of the cars' resale value and mitigates broader concerns of battery degradation.

9.2   Increasing Costs of Raw Materials

As demand for EVs grows and the supply of raw materials is stretched thin, the prices of raw materials are continuously increasing across the globe. The price of lithium, one of the most important components of the batteries used in EVs, rose nearly 500% in 2021, as shown in Fig. 9.1 (Kurmelovs 2022). Furthermore, the prices of cobalt and nickel also increased in 2021.

According to a report by AlixPartners, the costs of the raw material for an average EV totaled about EUR 8100 as of May 2022, up 144% from 3318 euros in March 2020 (Wayland 2022). Furthermore, the worldwide semiconductor shortage is becoming more and more problematic as demand increases due to the smartification and advancement of multiple industries. This increase in costs is not limited to just EVs; prices of raw materials for traditional ICE vehicles also increased by 106% between March 2020 and May 2022.

Several factors are causing the shortages in materials and increases in prices. One of them is the COVID-19 pandemic, which has caused countless supply chain issues and in turn delays in production and

Lithium Carbonate (CNY/T) 476500.0000000

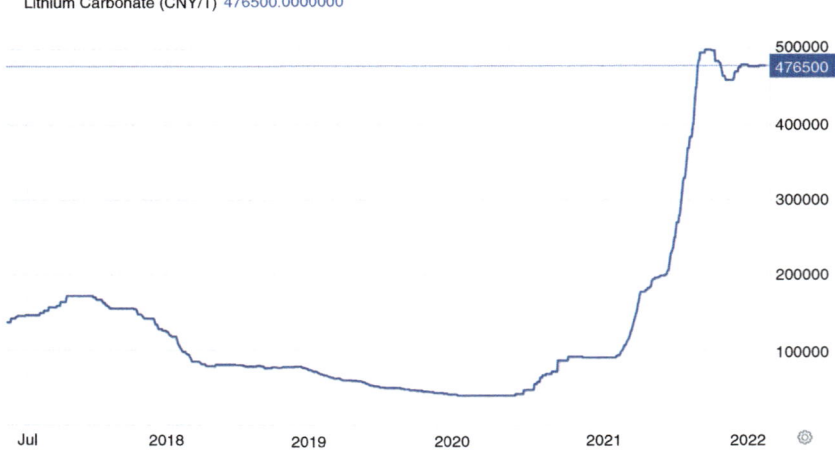

Fig. 9.1 Price of lithium in recent years (Trading Economics 2022)

manufacturing. Another factor is Russia's war in Ukraine, as both countries are sources of valuable raw materials. The most important factor, however, is the increase in demand. As sales of EVs continue to rise rapidly, the supply can no longer keep up with the demand. Automakers are scrambling to secure their supply and are willing to pay more for it, passing on the cost to their customers.

The increasing costs of raw materials are cutting into the margins for both automakers and suppliers, and forcing them to share these costs with consumers, as was the case when NIO raised its prices in April 2022. However, customers are reluctant to pay more for the same product. Automakers have to take into account that there is no way of avoiding this dilemma and plan production accordingly.

9.3   Governmental Regulations

Another issue that stands in the way of Chinese companies expanding internationally is the difference in governmental regulations between countries. While regulations in some countries may benefit Chinese automakers, such as by allowing autonomous driving technology to be developed quicker, the sheer variety of rules poses a huge challenge, as the companies have to adapt their cars and practices to each country they enter. Regulations differ in areas such as the safety standards of cars and data privacy regulations.

While Chinese automakers no longer have the reputation for being unsafe like they did a decade ago, data privacy and cybersecurity are becoming greater concerns due to the smartification of cars and the development of autonomous driving. In 2020, the World Forum for Harmonization of Vehicle Regulations, also known as WP.29, adopted two new United Nations regulations that establish clear performance and audit requirements related to cybersecurity for car manufacturers (UNECE 2020). The new regulations require that measures be implemented across four distinct disciplines:

- Managing vehicle cybersecurity risks
- Designing vehicles to secure them against risks along the value chain
- Detecting and responding to security incidents across the vehicle fleet
- Providing safe and secure software updates to ensure vehicle safety is not compromised and introducing a legal basis for the so-called over-the-air (OTA) updates to on-board vehicle software

Chinese automakers will have to pay close attention to these regulations' stringent requirements and integrate appropriate features into their cars.

Their problems are not just limited to overseas, however. As briefly mentioned in Sect. 3.3, ride-sharing giant Didi Chuxing ran into trouble with the Chinese government. Days after their initial public offering (IPO) on the New York Stock Exchange (NYSE), the Chinese government launched an unprecedented cybersecurity investigation into the company on national security grounds, pulling their apps from Chinese app stores (Pan 2022). Once in an unassailable position, Didi Chuxing has continuously lost users and market share since that investigation began.

Domestically, Chinese automakers must make sure they comply with the regulations set by their own government. Beijing has the final say within China and has no problem with taking drastic measures to rein in companies that are not aligned with their vision. This complicates any attempts of Chinese automakers to move overseas, as they then ought to appease two governments at the same time. The Chinese government is especially wary of Chinese companies going public, as such a move can result in other countries gaining access to confidential information.

9.4   Growing Competition

With the EV market growing rapidly as the world shifts toward more sustainable alternatives for transportation, more and more manufacturers are producing or considering producing their own EVs. Several of the EV stakeholders involved were covered in Chap. 3, including traditional automakers, automotive suppliers, Internet giants, and EV start-ups. Everyone wants their cut of the market, and Chinese automakers will have their work cut out to fend off the fierce competition from both their domestic counterparts and international juggernauts.

Although Tesla currently leads the pack when it comes to market share for BEVs, this could change in the next few years as the gap between the market leaders and their challengers will only shrink. BYD has already taken the lead in overall EVs (BEVs and PHEVs), and SAIC is hot on their heels. The range of EVs available to customers has increased steadily in recent years, as seen in Fig. 9.2 (IEA 2021), and the smallest detail can influence a customer's choice. The next development will likely be a race in research and development as each party strives to outdo its competition in terms of its vehicles' range, intelligence, and price, among other factors.

While Chinese automakers may enjoy some level of first-mover advantage thanks to the Chinese government's focus on the EV market, this is quickly shrinking as subsidies are being cut, and the rest of the world is catching up. Collaboration will be an important topic in the future, since knowledge needs to be shared if companies are going to speed up the innovation process. Traditional heavyweights like Volkswagen will not just stagnate; it is up to Chinese automakers to continue innovating to maintain their lead.

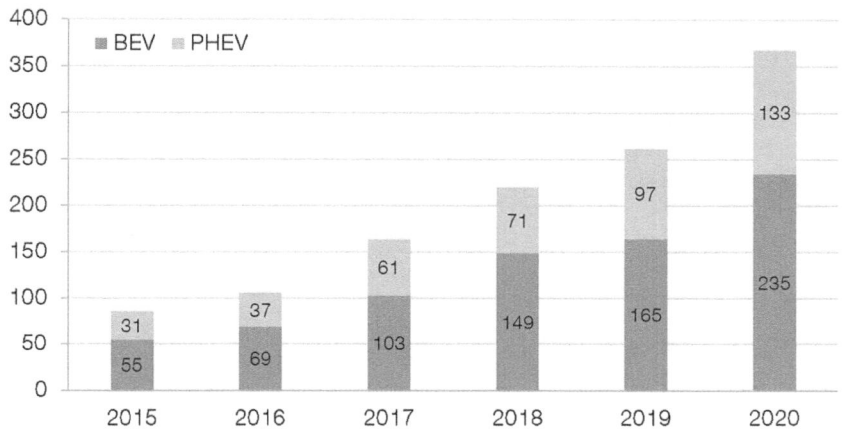

Fig. 9.2 Number of EV models available globally (IEA 2021)

References

IEA (2021) Electric car models available globally and average range, 2015–2020. https://www.iea.org/data-and-statistics/charts/electric-car-models-available-globally-and-average-range-2015-2020-2. Accessed 23 Aug 2022

Kurmelovs R (2022) 'Gone ballistic': lithium price rockets nearly 500% in a year amid electric vehicle rush. The Guardian. https://www.theguardian.com/australia-news/2022/feb/09/gone-ballistic-lithium-price-rockets-nearly-500-in-a-year-amid-electric-vehicle-rush. Accessed 23 Aug 2022

NIO (2022) An innovative smart power service solution. NIO website. https://www.NIO.com/baas. Accessed 23 Aug 2022

Pan C (2022) Chinese ride-hailing giant Didi still awaits final ruling from Beijing, one year after it was put under cybersecurity review. South China Morning Post. https://www.scmp.com/tech/big-tech/article/3183872/chinese-ride-hailing-giant-didi-still-awaits-final-ruling-beijing-one. Accessed 23 Aug 2022

Trading Economics (2022) Lithium. https://tradingeconomics.com/commodity/lithium. Accessed 23 Aug 2022

UNECE (2020) UN regulations on cybersecurity and software updates to pave the way for mass roll out of connected vehicles. UNECE Press Releases. https://unece.org/sustainable-development/press/un-regulations-cybersecurity-and-software-updates-pave-way-mass-roll. Accessed 23 Aug 2022

Wayland M (2022) Raw material costs for electric vehicles have doubled during the pandemic. CNBC. https://www.cnbc.com/2022/06/22/electric-vehicle-raw-material-costs-doubled-during-pandemic.html. Accessed 23 Aug 2022

Zhou J (2021) 贬值率是燃油车3倍 新能源车保值率调查 (Depreciation rate is three times the fuel car: new energy car value preservation rate survey). Geeknev.com https://www.geeknev.com/news/293/2939679.html. Accessed 23 Aug 2022

10

What the Future Has in Store

Keywords Electric vehicle industry • Automotive industry • Globalia • Chinese automakers

One thing is for sure—the future looks rosy for the EV industry. Driven by climate change, improving technology, and rising fuel costs, the adoption of EVs is accelerating across the world. EV sales more than doubled in 2021, and the global market share of EVs is increasing rapidly. While Tesla still retains the lead in the BEV category, Chinese automakers have overtaken Tesla in overall EV sales, with BYD leading the charge.

The Chinese government has now taken a step back, since it views the EV market as mature enough to drive its own growth. Many EV stakeholders are making moves and innovating within the automotive industry to claim their share of the market. The automotive industry is no longer limited to just automakers, as suppliers and mobility providers are playing increasingly large roles.

Technology within the EV industry will only continue to improve, particularly battery life, thus alleviating one of the main obstacles to

© The Author(s), under exclusive license to Springer Nature Switzerland AG 2023
J. Y. Yang et al., *Chinese Electric Vehicle Trailblazers*, Business Guides on the Go,
https://doi.org/10.1007/978-3-031-25145-0_10

adoption—range anxiety. In addition, improvements in charging infrastructure and innovative initiatives such as NIO's BaaS model will encourage more drivers to purchase EVs.

However, these improvements are not limited to just the electrification of cars. In the new age of the electric vehicle, smartification is the holy grail for Chinese automakers. EV intelligence is one of the main ways Chinese automakers differentiate themselves from their competitors, as they strive to turn the EV into a smart, multifunctional terminal. They have embraced the mobile era and begun adding countless features to EVs to improve the user experience, culminating with autonomous driving.

The strategies employed by these Chinese automakers are strikingly different from those used in Europe or the USA, in sales, marketing, or pricing. The transactional business model is slowly becoming outdated as Chinese automakers look for new ways to enhance and extend the customer journey.

The mobile era has given rise to several strategies involving fan economy and gamification, and Chinese automakers are taking advantage of these to market their EVs to customers. These methods and the companies' understanding of the Chinese market have allowed them to take back domestic market share from international automakers such as Volkswagen and Toyota.

Chinese automakers put great emphasis on customers, tailoring their products to consumers' needs and pricing them in line with their willingness to pay. For example, NIO opts for premium pricing, while SGMW sets an extremely low price for the Wuling Hongguang Mini. Chinese automakers also generate income for the lifetime of the EV by offering an extended customer journey, and some are beginning to realize the attractiveness of offering flexible pricing models, choosing to offer subscription-based services for various features to their customers.

The next step for Chinese automakers is to translate their success in the domestic market into international markets. Many are yet to begin expanding overseas, but among those that have, there are positive signs that they have learned from past failed efforts. Nevertheless, they will certainly have to face more challenges on the march to Globalia, such as the increasing costs of raw materials and the differences in governmental regulations and standards between countries.

The era of ICE vehicles is coming to a close. In the era of electric vehicles, Chinese automakers have established themselves as the trailblazers of the automotive industry, and it is only a matter of time before the rest of the world starts to take notice.

Glossary of Abbreviations and Acronyms

ADaaS	Autonomous driving as a service
ADAS	Advanced driver assistance systems
AI	Artificial intelligence
BaaS	Battery as a service
BEV	Battery electric vehicle
CAFC	Corporate average fuel consumption
CAGR	Compound annual growth rate
C-V2X	Cellular vehicle-to-everything
DL	Deep learning
EREV	Extended-range electric vehicle
EV	Electric vehicle
FCEV	Fuel cell electric vehicle
FSD	Full self-driving
GDP	Gross domestic product
HEV	Hybrid electric vehicle
HMI	Human–machine interface
ICE	Internal combustion engine
IPO	Initial public offering
IVI	In-vehicle infotainment
KFC	Kentucky Fried Chicken

© The Author(s), under exclusive license to Springer Nature Switzerland AG 2023
J. Y. Yang et al., *Chinese Electric Vehicle Trailblazers*, Business Guides on the Go,
https://doi.org/10.1007/978-3-031-25145-0

KOC	Key opinion consumer
KOL	Key opinion leader
kW	Kilowatt
kWh	Kilowatt-hour
MHEV	Mild hybrid electric vehicle
MIIT	Ministry of Industry and Information Technology
MVP	Minimum viable product
NDRC	National Development and Reform Commission
NEV	New energy vehicle
NMC	Nickel manganese cobalt
NYSE	New York Stock Exchange
OS	Operating system
OTA	Over-the-air
PHEV	Plug-in hybrid electric vehicle
R&D	Research and development
RMB	Renminbi
SAE	Society of Automotive Engineers
SPAC	Special-purpose acquisition company
TOPS	Trillion operations per second
UGC	User-generated content
UN	United Nations
USD	US dollar
V2X	Vehicle-to-everything
ZEV	Zero-emissions vehicle

Index